DEATH IN VENICE

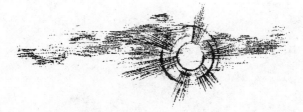

MODERN LIBRARY COLLEGE EDITIONS

DEATH IN VENICE

by THOMAS MANN

A revised edition of the authorized translation

by KENNETH BURKE

With a critical essay by ERICH HELLER

NORTHWESTERN UNIVERSITY

New York / THE MODERN LIBRARY
Distributed by McGraw-Hill, Inc.

THE MODERN LIBRARY
is published by Random House, Inc.

Manufactured in the United States of America

Autobiography and Literature

A critical essay on Death in Venice *that should be read after the first and before the second reading of the book.*

BY *Erich Heller*

(This essay appears at the back of this edition following the text.)

DEATH IN VENICE

I

On a spring afternoon of the year 19—, when for several months the situation in Europe had been so menacing, Gustav Aschenbach, or von Aschenbach as his name read officially after his fiftieth birthday, had left his residence on the Prinzregentenstrasse in Munich and had gone for a long walk. Overwrought by the trying and precarious work of the forenoon—which had demanded a maximum wariness, prudence, penetration, and rigor of the will—the writer had not been able even after the noon meal to break the impetus of the productive mechanism within him, that *motus animi continuus* which constitutes, according to Cicero, the foundation of eloquence; and he had not attained the healing sleep which—what with the increasing exhaustion of his strength—he needed in the middle of each day. So he had gone outdoors soon after tea, in the hopes that air and movement would restore him and prepare him for a profitable evening.

It was the beginning of May, and after cold, damp weeks a false midsummer had set in. The English Gardens, although the foliage was still fresh and sparse, were as pungent as in August, and in the parts nearer the city had been full of conveyances and promenaders. At the Aumeister, which he had reached by quieter and quieter paths, Aschenbach had surveyed for a short time the garden restaurant with its lively crowds and its border of cabs and carriages. From here, as the sun was sinking, he had started home, outside the park, across the open fields; and since he felt tired and a storm was threatening from the direction of Föhring, he waited at the North Cemetery for the tram which would take him directly back to the city.

It happened that he found no one at the tram stop or in its vicinity. There was not a vehicle to be seen, either on the paved Ungererstrasse, with its solitary glistening rails stretching out toward Schwabing, or on the Föhringer Chaussee. Behind the fences of the stonemasons' establishments, where the crosses, memorial tablets, and monuments standing for sale formed a second, uninhabited burial ground, there was no sign of life; and opposite him the Byzantine structure of the Funeral Hall lay silent in the reflection of the departing day, its façade ornamented in luminous colors with Greek crosses and hieratic paintings, above which were displayed inscriptions symmetrically arranged in gold letters, and texts chosen to bear on the life beyond, such as "They enter into the dwelling of the Lord" or "The light of eternity shall shine upon them." And for some time, as he stood waiting, he found a grave diversion in

spelling out the formulas and letting his mind's eye
lose itself in their transparent mysticism, when, returning from his reveries, he noticed in the portico, above
the two apocalyptic animals guarding the steps, a man
whose somewhat unusual appearance gave his thoughts
an entirely new direction.

Whether he had just now come out from the inside
through the bronze door, or had approached and
mounted from the outside unobserved, remained uncertain. Aschenbach, without applying himself especially to the matter, was inclined to believe the former.
Of medium height, thin, smooth-shaven, and noticeably
pug-nosed, the man belonged to the red-haired type and
possessed the appropriate milky, freckled complexion.
Obviously, he was not of Bavarian extraction. since at
least the white and straight-brimmed straw hat that
covered his head gave his appearance the stamp of a
foreigner, of someone who had come from a long distance. To be sure, he was wearing the customary knapsack strapped across his shoulders, and a belted suit of
rough yellow wool; his left forearm was propped against
his waist, and his gray storm cape was thrown across it.
In his right hand, diagonally to the ground, he held a
stick with an iron ferrule, while, with his feet crossed,
he was leaning his hip against the crook. His head was
raised so that the Adam's apple protruded hard and
bare on a scrawny neck emerging from a loose sport
shirt. And he was staring sharply off into the distance,
with colorless, red-lidded eyes between which stood two
strong, vertical wrinkles that made a strange contrast
with his short, turned-up nose. Thus—and perhaps his
elevated position helped to give the impression—his
bearing had something majestic and commanding about

it, something bold, or even savage. For whether he was grimacing because he was blinded by the setting sun, or whether it was a case of a permanent distortion of the physiognomy, his lips seemed too short, they were so completely pulled back from his teeth that these were exposed even to the gums, and stood out white and long.

It is quite possible that Aschenbach, in his half-distracted, half-inquisitive examination of the stranger, had been somewhat inconsiderate, for he suddenly became aware that his look was being answered, and indeed so militantly, so straight in the eye, so plainly with the intention of driving the thing through to the very end and compelling him to capitulate, that he turned away uncomfortably and began walking along by the fences, deciding casually that he would pay no further attention to the man. The next minute he had forgotten him. But perhaps the exotic element in the stranger's appearance had worked on his imagination; or a new physical or spiritual influence of some sort had come into play. He was quite astonished to note a peculiar inner expansion, a kind of roving unrest, a youthful longing after far-off places: a feeling so vivid, so new, or so long dormant and neglected, that, with his hands behind his back and his eyes on the ground, he came to a sudden stop, and peered into the nature and purport of this emotion.

It was the desire for travel, nothing more; although, to be sure, it had attacked him violently, and was heightened to a passion, even to the point of a hallucination. His yearnings took visual form; his imagination, still in ferment from his hours of work, actually pictured all the marvels and terrors of a manifold world which it was suddenly struggling to conceive. He saw a landscape, a tropical swampland under a heavy, murky sky, damp, luxuriant and enormous, a kind of primeval wilderness of islands, bogs, and arms of water, sluggish with mud; he saw, near him and in the distance, the hairy shafts of palms rising out of a rank voluptuous thicket, out of places where the plant life was fat, swollen, and blossoming exorbitantly; he saw strangely misshapen trees lowering their roots into the ground, into stagnant pools with greenish reflections; and here, between floating flowers which were milk-white and large as dishes, birds of a strange nature, high-shouldered, with crooked bills, were standing in the muck, and looking motionlessly to one side; between dense, knotted stalks of bamboo he saw the glint from the eyes of a crouching tiger—and he felt his heart knock with fear and with puzzled desires. Then the image disappeared; and with a shake of his head Aschenbach resumed his walk along past the fences of the stone-masons' establishments.

Since the time, at least, when he could command the means to enjoy the advantages of moving about the world as he pleased, he had considered traveling simply as a hygienic precaution which must be complied with now and then despite one's feelings and one's preferences. Too busy with the tasks arranged for him by his interest in his own ego and in the problems of Europe, too burdened with the onus of production, too little prone to diversion to be attracted by the varied amusements of the great world, he had been thoroughly satisfied with such knowledge of the earth's surface as anyone can get without moving far out of his own circle; and he had never even been tempted to leave Europe. Especially now that his life was slowly on the decline, and that the artist's fear of not having finished—this uneasiness lest the clock run down before he had done his part and given himself completely—could no longer be waved aside as a mere whim, he had confined his outer existence almost exclusively to the beautiful city which had become his home and to the rough country house which he had built in the mountains and where he spent the rainy summers.

Further, this thing which had laid hold of him so belatedly, but with such suddenness, was very readily moderated and adjusted by the force of his reason and of a discipline which he had practiced since youth. He had intended carrying to a certain point the work for which he now lived before moving to the country. And the thought of knocking about the world for months while neglecting his work seemed much too lax and contrary to his plans; it really could not be considered seriously. Yet he knew only too well what the reasons were for this unexpected temptation. It was the urge to escape—he admitted to himself—this yearning for the new and the remote, this appetite for freedom, for unburdening, for forgetfulness; it was a pressure away from his work, from the steady drudgery of a coldly passionate service. To be sure, he loved this work and almost loved the enervating battle that was fought daily between a proud tenacious will—so often tested— and this growing weariness which no one was to suspect and which must not betray itself in his productions by any sign of weakness or negligence. But it seemed wise not to draw the bow overtightly, and not to strangle by sheer obstinacy so strongly persistent an appetite. He thought of his work, thought of the place at which yesterday and now again today he had been forced to

leave off, and which, it seemed, would yield neither to
patience and coaxing nor to a definite attack. He ex-
amined it again, trying to break through or to circum-
vent the deadlock, but he gave up with a shudder of
repugnance. There was no unusual difficulty here; what
balked him was the scruples of aversion, which took
the form of a fastidious insatiability. Even as a young
man this insatiability had meant to him the very nature,
the fullest essence, of talent; and for that reason he had
restrained and chilled his emotions, since he was aware
that they incline to content themselves with a happy
approximate, a state of semicompletion. Were these
enslaved emotions now taking their vengeance on him
by leaving him in the lurch, by refusing to forward and
accelerate his art; and were they bearing off with them
every enjoyment, every live interest in form and
expression?

Not that he was producing anything bad; his years
gave him at least this advantage, that he felt himself
at all times in full and easy possession of his craftsmanship. But while the nation honored him for this, he himself was not content; and it seemed to him that his work
lacked those marks of fiery, sportive emotionalism which,
themselves the fruits of joy, and more direct in their
appeal than any depth of content, set the conditions for
the delight of an appreciative public. He feared the
summer in the country, alone in the little house with
the maid who prepared his meals, and the servant
who brought them to him. He feared the familiar view
of the mountain peaks and the slopes which would
stand about him in his boredom and his discontent.
Consequently there was need of a break in some new
direction. If the summer was to be endurable and

productive, he must attempt something out of his usual orbit; he must relax, get a change of air, bring an element of freshness into the blood. To travel, then —that much was settled. Not far, not all the way to the tigers. But one night on the sleeper, and a rest of three or four weeks at some pleasant popular resort in the South. . . .

He thought this out while the noise of the electric tram came nearer along the Ungererstrasse; and as he boarded it, he decided to devote the evening to the study of maps and timetables. On the platform it occurred to him to look around for the man in the straw hat, his companion during that not exactly inconsequential time he had spent waiting. But his whereabouts remained uncertain, as he was not to be seen either at the place where he was formerly standing, or anywhere else in the vicinity of the tram stop, or on the car itself.

II

THE author of that lucid and powerful prose epic built around the life of Frederick of Prussia; the tenacious artist who, with sustained application, wove rich, varied strands of human destiny together under one single predominating theme in the fictional tapestry known as *Maya*; the creator of that stark tale which is called *The Wretch* and which pointed out for a grateful oncoming generation the possibility of some moral certainty beyond pure knowledge; finally, the writer (and this sums up briefly the works of his mature period) of the impassioned treatise on "Art and the Spirit," whose capacity for mustering facts, and, further, whose fluency in their presentation, led cautious judges to place this treatise alongside Schiller's conclusions on naïve and sentimental poetry—Gustav Aschenbach, then, was the son of a higher law official, and was born in L——, a leading city in the province of Silesia. His forebears had been officers, magistrates, government functionaries, men who had led severe, steady lives serving their king, their state. A deeper strain of spirituality had been manifest in them once, in the person of a preacher; the preceding generation had brought a brisker, more sensuous blood into the family through the author's mother, daughter of a Bohemian bandmaster. The traces of foreignness in his features came from her. A marriage of sober, painstaking conscientiousness with impulses of a darker, more fiery nature had had an artist as its result, and this particular artist.

Since his whole nature was centered on acquiring a reputation, he showed himself, if not exactly precocious, at least (thanks to the firmness and pithiness of his personality, his accent) ripened and adjusted to the public at an early age. Almost as a schoolboy he had made a name for himself. Within ten years he had learned to face the world through the medium of his writing table, to discharge the obligations of his fame in a correspondence which (since many claims are pressed on the successful, the trustworthy) had to be brief as well as pleasant and to the point. At forty, wearied by the vicissitudes and the exertion of his own work, he had to manage a daily mail which bore the postmarks of countries in all parts of the world.

Equally removed from the banal and the eccentric, his talents were so constituted as to gain both the confidence of the general public and the admiring and exacting sympathy of the critical. Thus even as a young man continually devoted to the pursuit of craftsmanship—and that of no ordinary kind—he had never known the careless freedom of youth. When, around thirty-five years of age, he had been taken ill in Vienna, one sharp observer said of him in company: "You see, Aschenbach has always lived like this," and the speaker contracted the fingers of his left hand into a fist; "never like this," and he let his open hand droop comfortably from the arm of his chair. That hit the mark; and the moral heroism of it was that he was not of a strong constitution, and though he was pledged by his nature to these steady efforts, he was not really born to them.

Considerations of ill health had kept him from attending school as a boy, and had compelled him to receive instruction at home. He had grown up alone, without comrades—and he was forced to realize soon enough that he belonged to a race which often lacked, not talent, but that physical substructure which talent relies on for its fullest fruition: a race accustomed to giving its best early, and seldom extending its faculties over the years. But his favorite phrase was "carrying through"; in his novel on Frederick he saw the pure apotheosis of this command, which struck him as the essential concept of the virtuous in action and passion. Also, he wished earnestly to grow old, since he had always maintained that the only artistry which can be called truly great, comprehensive—yes, even truly admirable—is that which is permitted to bear fruits characteristic of each stage in human development.

Since he must carry the responsibilities of his talent on frail shoulders, and wanted to go a long way, the primary requirement was discipline—and fortunately discipline was his direct inheritance from his father's side. By forty, fifty, or at an earlier age when others are still slashing about with enthusiasm, and are confidently putting off to some later date the execution of plans on a large scale, he would start the day early, dashing cold water over his chest and back, and then, with a couple of tall wax candles in silver candlesticks at the head of his manuscript, he would expend on his art, in two or three eager, scrupulous morning hours, the strength which he had accumulated in sleep. It was pardonable, indeed it was a direct tribute to the effectiveness of his moral scheme, that the uninitiated took his *Maya* world, and the massive epic machinery upon which the life of the hero Frederick was unrolled, as evidence of long breath and sustaining power. While actually they had been built up layer by layer, in small daily allotments, through hundreds and hundreds of single inspirations. And if they were so excellent in both composition and texture, it was solely because their creator had held out for years under the strain of one single work, with a steadiness of will and a tenacity comparable to that which conquered his native province; and because, finally, he had turned over his most vital and valuable hours to the strains of production.

In order that a significant work of the mind may exert immediately some broad and deep effect, a secret re-

14

lationship, or even conformity, must exist between the
personal destiny of the author and the common destiny
of his contemporaries. People do not know why they
raise a work of art to fame. Far from being connoisseurs,
they believe that they see in it hundreds of virtues
which justify so much interest; but the true reason for
their applause is an unconscious sympathy. Aschenbach
had once stated quite plainly in some inconspicuous
place that nearly everything great which comes into
being does so in spite of something—in spite of sorrow
or suffering, poverty, destitution, physical weakness,
depravity, passion, or a thousand other handicaps. But
that was not merely an observation; it was a discovery,
the formula of his life and reputation, the key to his
work. And what wonder, then, that it was also the
distinguishing moral trait, the dominating gesture, of
his most characteristic figures?

Years before, one shrewd analyst had written of the
new hero type to which this author gave preference,
and which kept turning up in variations of one sort or
another: he called it the conception of "an intellectual
and youthful masculinity" which "stands motionless,
haughty, ashamed, with jaw set, while swords and spear
points pierce the body." That was beautiful and ingen-
ious; and it was exact, although it may have seemed to
suggest too much passivity. For to be poised against
fatality, to meet adverse conditions gracefully, is more
than simple endurance; it is an act of aggression, a
positive triumph—and the figure of Sebastian is the
most beautiful figure, if not of art as a whole, at least
of the art of literature. Looking into this fictional world,
one saw: a delicate self-mastery by which any inner
deterioration, any biological decay, was kept concealed

from the eyes of the world; a crude, vicious sensuality capable of fanning its rising passions into pure flame, yes, even of mounting to dominance in the realm of beauty; a pallid weakness which draws from the glowing depths of the soul the strength to bow whole arrogant peoples before the foot of the cross, or before the feet of weakness itself; a charming manner maintained in his cold, strict service to form; a false, precarious mode of living, and the keenly enervating melancholy and artifice of the born deceiver—to observe such trials as this was enough to make one question whether there really was any heroism other than weakness. And, in any case, what heroism could be more in keeping with the times? Gustav Aschenbach was the one poet among the many workers on the verge of exhaustion: the over-burdened, the used-up, the clingers-on, in short all those moralists of production who, delicately built and destitute of means, can rely for a time at least on will power and the shrewd husbandry of their resources to secure the effect of greatness. There are many such: they are the heroes of the period. And they all found themselves in his works; here they were indeed, upheld, intensified, applauded; they were grateful to him, they acclaimed him.

In his time he had been young and raw; and, misled by his age, he had blundered in public. He had stumbled, had exposed himself; both in writing and in talk he had offended against caution and tact. But he had acquired the dignity which, as he insisted, is the innate goad and craving of every great talent; in fact, it could be said that his entire development had been a conscious undeviating progression away from the embarrassments of skepticism and irony, and toward dignity.

The general masses are satisfied by vigor and tangibility of treatment rather than by any close intellectual processes; but youth, with its passion for the absolute, can be arrested only by the problematical. And Aschenbach had been absolute, problematical, as only a youth could be. He had been a slave to the intellect, had played havoc with knowledge, had ground up his seed crops, had divulged secrets, had discredited talent, had betrayed art—yes, while his modelings were entertaining the faithful votaries, filling them with enthusiasm, making their lives more keen, this youthful artist was taking the breath away from the generation then in its twenties by his cynicisms on the questionable nature of art, and of artistry itself.

But it seems that nothing blunts the edge of a noble, robust mind more quickly and more thoroughly than the sharp and bitter stimulus of knowledge; and certainly the moody radicalism of the youth, no matter how conscientious, was shallow in comparison with his firm determination as an older man and a master to deny knowledge, to reject it, to pass it with raised head, insofar as it is capable of crippling, discouraging, or degrading to the slightest degree, our will, acts, feelings, or even passions. How else could the famous story *The Wretch* be understood than as an outburst of repugnance against the indecent psychologism of the times: embodied in the figure of that soft and stupid half-clown who pilfers a destiny for himself by guiding his wife (from powerlessness, from lasciviousness, from ethical frailty) into the arms of an adolescent, and believes that he may through profundity commit vileness? The power of the word with which he here cast out the outcast announced the turn away from all moral skepticism, all sympathy with the abyss; it was the counter-move to the laxity of the sympathetic principle that to understand all is to forgive all—and the thing that was here well begun, even nearly completed. was that "miracle of reborn ingenuousness" which was taken up a little later in one of the author's dialogues expressly and not without a certain discreet emphasis. Strange coincidences! Was it as a result of this rebirth, this new dignity and sternness, that his feeling for beauty—a discriminating purity, simplicity, and evenness of attack which henceforth gave his productions such an obvious, even such a deliberate stamp of mastery and classicism—showed an almost excessive strengthening about this time? But ethical resoluteness beyond knowledge, the knowledge that corrodes or inhibits moral firmness—does this not in turn signify a simplification, a reduction morally of the world to too limited terms, and thus also a strengthened capacity for the forbidden, the evil, the morally impossible? And does not form have two aspects? Is it not moral and amoral at once—moral in that it is the result and expression of discipline, but amoral, and even immoral, in that by nature it contains an indifference to morality, is calculated, in fact, to make morality bend beneath its proud and unencumbered scepter?

Be that as it may. An evolution is a destiny; and why should his evolution, which had been upheld by the general confidence of a vast public, not run through a course different from one consummated without the luster and entanglements of fame? Only chronic vagabondage will find it tedious and be inclined to scoff when a great talent outgrows the lax preparatory stage, learns to seize upon and express the dignity of the

mind, and imposes a formal etiquette upon a solitude
which had been filled with unaided, starkly isolated
straining and struggling, and eventually had acquired
power and honor among men. Further, how much sport,
defiance, indulgence there is in the self-formation of a
talent! Gradually something official, didactic, crept into
Gustav Aschenbach's productions, his style in later life
fought shy of any abruptness and boldness, any subtle
and unexpected shadings; he inclined toward the fixed
and standardized, the conventionally elegant, the
conservative, the formal, the formulated, nearly. And,
as is traditionally said of Louis XIV, with the advancing
years he came to omit every common word from his
vocabulary. At about this time it happened that the
educational authorities included selected pages by him
in their prescribed school readers. This was deeply
sympathetic to his nature, and he did not decline when
a German prince who had just mounted the throne
raised the author of the "Frederick" to knighthood on
the occasion of his fiftieth birthday. After a few years
of unrest, a few tentative stopping places here and
there, he soon chose Munich as his permanent home,
and lived there in a state of high repute, such as, in
exceptional cases, is accorded the life of the mind. The
marriage which, when still young, he had contracted
with a girl of an educated family came to an end with
her death after a short period of happiness. He was left
with a daughter, now married. He had never had
a son.

Gustav von Aschenbach was somewhat below average
height, dark, and smooth-shaven. His head seemed a
bit too large in comparison with his almost dapper
figure. His hair was brushed straight back, thinning out

toward the crown, but very full about the temples, and strongly marked with gray; it framed a high, ridged forehead. Gold spectacles with rimless lenses cut into the bridge of his bold, heavy nose. The mouth was big, sometimes drooping, sometimes suddenly pinched and firm. His cheeks were thin and wrinkled, his well-formed chin had a slight cleft. This head, usually bent patiently to one side, seemed to have been through momentous experiences, and yet it was his art which had produced those effects in his face, effects which are elsewhere the result of hard and tense living. Behind this brow the brilliant repartee of the dialogue on war between Voltaire and the king had been born; these eyes, peering steadily and wearily from behind their glasses, had seen the bloody inferno of the lazarets in the Seven Years' War. Even as it applies to the individual, art is a heightened mode of existence. It gives deeper pleasures, it consumes more quickly. It carves upon the faces of its votaries the marks of imaginary and spiritual adventures; and though their external existence may be as quiet as a monk's, in the long run it produces a fastidiousness, over-refinement, fatigue, and alertness of the nerves such as would not result from actual living, even if crammed with illicit passions and pleasures.

III

VARIOUS matters of a literary and social nature delayed his departure until about two weeks after that walk in Munich. Finally he gave orders to have his country house ready for occupancy within a month; and one day between the middle and the end of May he took the night train for Trieste, where he made a stopover of only twenty-four hours, and embarked the following morning for Pola.

What he was seeking was something alien and disrelated to his usual life which would at the same time be quickly within reach; and so he stopped at an island in the Adriatic which had become well known in recent years. It lay not far off the Istrian coast, with beautifully rugged cliffs fronting the open sea, and natives who dressed in variegated tatters and made strange sounds when they spoke. But rain and a heavy atmosphere, a provincial and exclusively Austrian patronage at the hotel, and the lack of that restfully intimate association with the sea which can be gotten only by a soft, sandy beach, irritated him, and prevented him from feeling that he had found the place he was looking for. Something within was disturbing him, and drawing him he was not sure where. He studied sailing dates, he looked about him questioningly, and of a sudden, as a thing both astounding and self-evident, his goal was before him. If you wanted to reach overnight the unique, the fabulously different, where did you go? But that was plain. What was he doing here? He had lost the trail. He had wanted to go there. He did not delay in giving notice as to his mistake in stopping here. In the early morning mist, a week and a half after his arrival on the island, a fast motorboat was carrying him and his luggage back over the water to the naval port, and he landed there just long enough to cross the gangplank to the damp deck of a ship which was lying under steam ready for the voyage to Venice.

It was an old hulk flying the Italian flag, decrepit, sooty, and mournful. In a cavelike, artificially lighted inside cabin where Aschenbach, immediately upon boarding the ship, was conducted by a dirty hunch-backed sailor, who smirked politely, there was sitting behind a table, his hat cocked over his forehead and a cigarette stump in the corner of his mouth, a man with a goatee, and with the face of an old-style circus direc-tor, who was taking down the particulars of the passen-gers with professional grimaces and distributing the tickets. "To Venice!" He repeated Aschenbach's re-quest, as he extended his arm and plunged his pen into the pasty dregs of a precariously tilted inkwell. "To Venice, first class! At your service, sir." And he wrote a generous scrawl, sprinkled it with blue sand out of a box, let the sand run off into a clay bowl, folded the paper with sallow, bony fingers, and began writing again. "A happily chosen destination!" he chatted on. "Ah, Venice! A splendid city! A city of irresistible attractiveness for the educated on account of its history as well as its present-day charms." The smooth rapidity of his movements and the empty words accompanying them had something anaesthetic and reassuring about them, much as though he feared lest the traveler might still be vacillating in his decision to go to Venice. He handled the cash briskly, and let the change fall on the spotted table cover with the skill of a croupier. "A pleasant journey, sir!" he said with a theatrical bow. "Gentlemen, I have the honor of serving you!" he called out immediately after, with his arm upraised, and he acted as if business were in full swing, although no one else was there to require his attention. Aschenbach returned to the deck.

With one arm on the railing, he watched the passengers on board and the idlers who loitered around the dock waiting for the ship to sail. The second-class passengers, men and women, were huddled together on the foredeck, using boxes and bundles as seats. A group of young people made up the travelers on the first deck, clerks from Pola, it seemed, who had gathered in high spirits for an excursion to Italy. They made a considerable fuss about themselves and their enterprise, chattered, laughed, enjoyed their own antics self-contentedly, and, leaning over the hand rails, shouted flippantly and mockingly at their comrades who, with portfolios under their arms, were going up and down the waterfront on business and kept threatening the picnickers with their canes. One, in a bright yellow summer suit of ultra-fashionable cut, with a red necktie, and a rakishly tilted Panama, surpassed all the others in his crowing good humor. But as soon as Aschenbach looked at him a bit more carefully, he discovered with a kind of horror that the youth was a cheat. He was old, that was unquestionable. There were wrinkles

around his eyes and mouth. The faint crimson of the
cheeks was paint, the hair under his brilliantly decorated straw hat was a wig; his neck was hollow and
stringy, his turned-up mustache and the imperial on his
chin were dyed; the full set of yellow teeth which he
displayed when he laughed, a cheap artificial plate; and
his hands, with signet rings on both index fingers, were
those of an old man. Fascinated with loathing, Aschenbach watched him in his intercourse with his friends.
Did they not know, did they not observe that he was
old, that he was not entitled to wear their bright, fop-
pish clothing, that he was not entitled to play at being
one of them? Unquestioningly, and as quite the usual
thing, it seemed, they allowed him among them, treat-
ing him as one of their own kind and returning his jovial
nudges in the ribs without repugnance. How could that
be? Aschenbach laid his hand on his forehead and closed
his eyes; they were hot, since he had had too little sleep.
He felt as though everything were not quite the same
as usual, as though some dreamlike estrangement, some
peculiar distortion of the world, were beginning to take
possession of him, and perhaps this could be stopped if
he hid his face for a time and then looked around him
again. Yet at this moment he felt as though he were
swimming; and, looking up with an unreasoned fear, he
discovered that the heavy, lugubrious body of the ship
was separating slowly from the walled bank. Inch by
inch, with the driving and reversing of the engine, the
strip of dirty glistening water widened between the dock
and the side of the ship; and, after cumbersome maneu-
vering, the steamer finally turned its nose toward the
open sea. Aschenbach crossed to the starboard side,
where the hunchback had set up a deck chair for him,

and a steward in a spotted dress coat asked after his wants.

The sky was gray, the wind damp. Harbor and islands had been left behind, and soon all land was lost in the haze. Flakes of coal dust, bloated with moisture, fell over the washed deck, which would not dry. After the first hour an awning was spread, since it had begun to rain.

Bundled up in his coat, a book in his lap, the traveler rested, and the hours passed unnoticed. It stopped raining; the canvas awning was removed. The horizon was unbroken. The sea, empty, like an enormous disk, lay stretched under the curve of the sky. But in empty inarticulate space our senses lose also the dimensions of time, and we slip into the incommensurate. As he rested, strange shadowy figures, the old dandy, the goatee from the inside cabin, passed through his mind, with vague gestures, muddled dream words—and he was asleep.

About noon he was called to a meal down in the corridorlike dining hall into which the doors opened from the sleeping cabins; he ate near the head of a long table, at the other end of which the clerks, including the old man, had been drinking with the boisterous captain since ten o'clock. The food was poor, and he finished rapidly. He felt driven outside to look at the sky, to see if it showed signs of being brighter above Venice.

He had kept thinking that this had to occur, since the city had always received him in full blaze. But sky and sea remained dreary and leaden, at times a misty rain fell, and he resigned himself to reaching by water a different Venice than he had ever found when approaching on land. He stood by the forestays, looking in the distance, waiting for land. He thought of the heavy-hearted, enthusiastic poet for whom the domes and bell towers of his dreams had once risen out of these waters; he relived in silence some of that reverence, happiness, and sorrow which had been turned then into measured song; and in response to a feeling that had already taken shape, he asked himself wearily and earnestly whether some new enchantment and distraction, some belated adventure of the emotions, might still be held in store for this idle traveler.

Then the flat coast emerged on the right; the sea was alive with fishing smacks; the bathers' island appeared; it dropped behind to the left, the steamer slowly entered the narrow port which is named after it; and on the lagoon, facing gay ramshackle houses, it stopped completely, since it had to wait for the barque of the health department.

An hour passed before it appeared. He had arrived, and yet he had not; no one was in any hurry, no one was driven by impatience. The young men from Pola, patriotically attracted by the military bugle calls which rang over the water from the vicinity of the public gardens, had come on deck and, warmed by their Asti, they burst out with cheers for the drilling *bersaglieri*. But it was repulsive to see what a state the primped-up old man had been brought to by his comradeship with youth. His old head was not able to resist its wine like the young and robust: he was painfully drunk. With glazed eyes, a cigarette between his trembling fingers, he stood in one place, swaying backward and forward from giddiness, and balancing himself laboriously. Since he would have fallen at the first step, he did not trust himself from the spot—yet he showed a deplorable insolence, buttonholed everyone who came near him, stammered, winked and tittered, lifted his wrinkled, ornamented index finger in a stupid attempt at bantering, while he licked the corners of his mouth with his tongue in the most abominably suggestive manner. Aschenbach observed him darkly, and a feeling of numbness came over him again, as though the world were displaying a faint but irresistible tendency to distort itself into the peculiar and the grotesque: a feeling which circumstances prevented him from surrendering himself to completely, for just then the pounding activity of the engines commenced again, and the ship, resuming a voyage which had been interrupted so near its completion, passed through the San Marco canal.

So he saw it again, the most remarkable of landing places, that blinding composition of fantastic buildings which the Republic lays out before the eyes of approaching seafarers: the soft splendor of the palace, the Bridge of Sighs, on the bank the columns with lion and saint, the advancing, showy flank of the enchanted temple, the glimpse through to the archway, and the giant clock. And as he looked on he thought that to reach Venice by land, on the railroad, was like entering a palace from the rear, and that this most unreal of cities should not be approached except as he was now doing, by ship, over the high seas.

The engine stopped, gondolas pressed in, the gangway was let down, customs officials climbed on board and discharged their duties perfunctorily; the disembarking could begin. Aschenbach made it understood that he wanted a gondola to take him and his luggage to the dock of those little steamers which ply between the city and the Lido, since he intended to locate near the sea. His plans were complied with, his wants were shouted down to the water, where the gondoliers were wrangling with one another in dialect. He was still hindered from descending; he was hindered by his trunk, which was being pulled and dragged with difficulty down the ladderlike steps—so that for some minutes he was not able to avoid the importunities of the atrocious old man, whose drunkenness gave him a sinister desire to do the foreigner parting honors. "We wish you a very agreeable visit," he bleated as he made an awkward bow. "May we commend ourselves to your most gracious memory? *Au revoir, excusez,* and *bon jour,* Your Excellency!" His mouth watered, he pressed his eyes shut, he licked the corners of his mouth, and the dyed imperial turned up about his senile lips. "Our compliments," he mumbled, with two fingertips on his mouth, "our compliments to the sweetheart, the dearest prettiest sweetheart . . ." And suddenly his false upper teeth fell down on his lower lip. Aschenbach was able to escape. "To the sweetheart, our handsome sweetheart," he heard the cooing, hollow, stuttering voice behind him while, supporting himself against the hand rail, he went down the gangway.

Who would not have to suppress a fleeting shudder, a vague timidity and uneasiness, if it were a matter of boarding a Venetian gondola for the first time or after several years? The strange craft, an entirely unaltered survival from the times of balladry, with that peculiar blackness which is found elsewhere only in coffins—it suggests silent, criminal adventures in the rippling night, it suggests even more strongly death itself, the bier and the mournful funeral, and the last silent journey. And has it been observed that the seat of such a barque, this armchair of coffin-black veneer and dull black upholstery, is the softest, most luxuriant, most lulling seat in the world? Aschenbach noted this when he had relaxed at the feet of the gondolier, opposite his luggage, which lay neatly assembled on the prow. The rowers were still wrangling, harshly, incomprehensibly, with threatening gestures. But the strange silence of this canal city seemed to soften their voices, to disembody them, and dissipate them over the water. It was warm here in the harbor. Touched faintly by the warm breeze of the sirocco, leaning back against the limber portions of the cushions, the traveler closed his eyes in the enjoyment of a lassitude which was as unusual with him as it was sweet. The trip would be short, he thought; if only it went on forever! He felt himself glide with a gentle motion away from the crowd and the confusion of voices.

It became quieter and quieter around him! There was nothing to be heard but the splashing of the oar, the hollow slapping of the waves against the prow of the boat as it stood above the water black and bold and armed with its halberdlike tip, and a third sound, of speaking, of whispering—the whispering of the gondolier, who was talking to himself between his teeth, fitfully, in words that were pressed out by the exertion of his arms. Aschenbach looked up, and was slightly astonished to discover that the lagoon was widening, and he was headed for the open sea. This seemed to indicate that he ought not to rest too much, but should see to it that his wishes were carried out.

"But it's to the steamer dock," he said, with a half-turn back. The muttering ceased. He got no answer.

"To the steamer dock!" he repeated, turning around completely and looking into the face of the gondolier who stood behind on a raised platform and towered up

between him and the dun-colored sky. He was a man of
unpleasant, even brutal appearance, dressed in sailor
blue, with a yellow sash; a formless straw hat, its weave
partially unraveled, was tilted insolently on his head.
The set of his face, the blond curly mustache beneath a
curtly turned-up nose, undoubtedly meant that he was
not Italian. Although of somewhat frail build, so that
one would not have thought him especially well suited
to his trade, he handled the oar with great energy,
throwing his entire body into each stroke. Occasionally
he drew back his lips from the exertion, and disclosed
his white teeth. Wrinkling his reddish brows, he gazed
on past his passenger, as he answered deliberately, almost gruffly: "You are going to the Lido." Aschenbach
replied: "Of course. But I have just taken the gondola
to get me across to San Marco. I want to use the
vaporetto."

"You cannot use the *vaporetto*, sir."

"And why not?"

"Because the *vaporetto* will not haul luggage."

That was so; Aschenbach remembered. He was silent.
But the fellow's harsh, presumptuous manner, so unusual toward a foreigner here, seemed unbearable. He
said: "That is my affair. Perhaps I want to put my
things in storage. You will turn back."

There was silence. The oar splashed, the water thud-
ded against the bow. And the talking and whispering
began again. The gondolier was talking to himself between his teeth.

What was to be done? This man was strangely insolent, and had an uncanny decisiveness; the traveler,
alone with him on the water, saw no way of getting what
he wanted. And besides, how softly he could rest, if
only he did not become excited! Hadn't he wanted the

trip to go on and on forever? It was wisest to let things take their course, and the main thing was that he was comfortable. The poison of inertia seemed to be issuing from the seat, from this low, black-upholstered armchair, so gently cradled by the oar strokes of the imperious gondolier behind him. The notion that he had fallen into the hands of a criminal passed dreamily across Aschenbach's mind—without the ability to summon his thoughts to an active defense. The possibility that it was all simply a plan for cheating him seemed more abhorrent. A feeling of duty or pride, a kind of recollection that one should prevent such things, gave him the strength to arouse himself once more. He asked: "What are you asking for the trip?"

Looking down upon him, the gondolier answered: "You will pay."

It was plain how this should be answered. Aschenbach said mechanically: "I shall pay nothing, absolutely nothing, if you don't take me where I want to go."

"You want to go to the Lido."

"But not with you."

"I am rowing you well."

That is so, Aschenbach thought, and relaxed. That is so; you are rowing me well. Even if you do have designs on my cash, and send me down to Pluto with a blow of your oar from behind, you will have rowed me well.

But nothing like that happened. They were even joined by others: a boatload of musical brigands, men and women, who sang to guitar and mandolin, riding persistently side by side with the gondola and filling the silence over the water with their covetous foreign poetry. A hat was held out, and Aschenbach threw in money. Then they stopped singing, and rowed away.

And again the muttering of the gondolier could be heard as he talked fitfully and jerkily to himself.

So they arrived, tossed in the wake of a steamer plying toward the city. Two municipal officers, their hands behind their backs, their faces turned in the direction of the lagoon, were walking back and forth on the bank. Aschenbach left the gondola at the dock, supported by that old man who is stationed with his grappling hook at each one of Venice's landing places. And since he had no small money, he crossed over to the hotel by the steamer wharf to get change and pay the rower what was due him. He got what he wanted in the lobby, he returned and found his traveling bags in a cart on the dock, and gondola and gondolier had vanished.

"He got out in a hurry," said the old man with the grappling hook. "A bad man, a man without a license, sir. He is the only gondolier who doesn't have a license. The others telephoned here."

Aschenbach shrugged his shoulders.

"The gentleman rode for nothing," the old man said, and held out his hat. Aschenbach tossed in a coin. He gave instructions to have his luggage taken to the Beach Hotel, and followed the cart through the avenue, the white-blossomed avenue which, lined on both sides with taverns, shops, and boarding houses, runs across the island to the shore.

He entered the spacious hotel from the rear, by the terraced garden, and passed through the vestibule and the lobby until he reached the desk. Since he had been announced, he was received with obliging promptness. A manager, a small, frail, flatteringly polite man with a black mustache and a French-style frock coat, accompanied him to the third floor in the lift, and showed him his room, an agreeable place furnished in cherry wood. It was decorated with strong-smelling flowers, and its high windows afforded a view out across the open sea. He stepped up to one of them after the employee had left; and while his luggage was being brought up and placed in the room behind him, he looked down on the beach (it was comparatively deserted in the afternoon) and on the sunless ocean which was at flood tide and was sending long low waves against the bank in a calm regular rhythm.

The experiences of a man who lives alone and in silence are both vaguer and more penetrating than those of people in society; his thoughts are heavier, more odd, and touched always with melancholy. Images and observations which could easily be disposed of by a glance, a smile, an exchange of opinion, will occupy him unbearably, sink deep into the silence, grow full of meaning, become life, adventure, emotion. Loneliness brings forth what is original, daringly and shockingly beautiful: the poetic. But loneliness also brings forth the perverse, the disproportionate, the absurd, and the illicit. So, the things he had met with on the trip, the ugly old fop with his twaddle about sweethearts, the lawbreaking gondolier who was cheated of his pay, still left the traveler uneasy. Without really providing any resistance to the mind, without offering any solid stuff to think over, they were nevertheless profoundly strange, as it seemed to him, and disturbing precisely because of this contradiction. In the meanwhile, he greeted the sea with his eyes, and felt pleasure at the knowledge that Venice was so conveniently near. Finally he turned away, bathed his face, left orders to the chambermaid for a few things he still needed done to make his comfort complete, and let himself be taken to the ground floor by the green-uniformed Swiss who operated the lift.

He took his tea on the terrace facing the ocean, then descended and followed the boardwalk for quite a way in the direction of the Hotel Excelsior. When he returned it seemed time to dress for dinner. He did this with his usual care and slowness, since he was accustomed to working over his toilet. And yet he came down a little early to the lobby, where he found a great many of the hotel guests assembled, mixing distantly and with a show of mutual indifference to one another, but all waiting for mealtime. He took a paper from the table, dropped into a leather chair, and observed the company; they differed agreeably from the guests where he had first stopped.

A wide and tolerantly inclusive horizon was spread out before him. Sounds of all the principal languages formed a subdued murmur. The accepted evening dress, a uniform of good manners, brought all human varieties into a fitting unity. There were Americans with their long wry features, large Russian families, English ladies, German children with French nurses. The Slavic element seemed to predominate. Polish was being spoken nearby.

It was a group of children gathered around a little wicker table, under the protection of a teacher or governess: three young girls, apparently fifteen to seventeen, and a long-haired boy about fourteen years old. With astonishment Aschenbach noted that the boy possessed perfect beauty. His face, pale and reserved, framed with honey-colored locks, the straight sloping nose, the lovely mouth, the expression of sweet and god-

like seriousness, recalled Greek sculpture of the noblest
period; and the complete purity of the forms was accompanied by such a rare personal charm that, as he
watched, he felt that he had never met with anything
equally felicitous in nature or the plastic arts. He was
further struck by the obviously intentional contrast
with the principles of upbringing which showed in the
sisters' attire and bearing. The three girls, the eldest
of whom could be considered grown up, were dressed
with a chasteness and severity bordering on disfigure-
ment. Uniformly cloisterlike costumes, of medium
length, slate-colored, sober, and deliberately unbecom-
ing in cut, with white turned-down collars as the only
relief, suppressed every possible appeal of shapeliness.
Their hair, brushed down flat and tight against the
head, gave their faces a nunlike emptiness and lack of
character. Surely this was a mother's influence, and it
had not even occurred to her to apply the pedagogical
strictness to the boy which she seemed to find necessary
for her girls. It was clear that in his existence the first
factors were gentleness and tenderness. The shears had
been resolutely kept from his beautiful hair; as with the
ancient statue of the "boy pulling out a thorn," it fell in
curls over his forehead, his ears, and still deeper, across
his neck. The English sailor suit, with its braids, stitch-
ings, and embroideries, its puffy sleeves narrowing at
the ends and fitting snugly about the fine wrists of his
still childish but slender hands, gave the delicate figure
something rich and luxurious. He was sitting, half-
profile to the observer, one foot in its black patent-
leather shoe placed before the other, an elbow resting
on the arm of his wicker chair, a cheek pressed against
his fist, in a position of negligent good manners, entirely

free of the almost subservient stiffness to which his
sisters seemed accustomed. Did he have some illness?
For his skin stood out as white as ivory against the
golden darkness of the surrounding curls. Or was he
simply a pampered favorite child, made this way by a
doting and moody love? Aschenbach inclined to believe
the latter. Almost every artist is born with a lush and
treasonous tendency to look with tolerance upon injus-
tices which have created beauty, and to meet aristocratic advantages with sympathy and reverence.

A waiter passed through and announced in English
that the meal was ready. Gradually the guests disappeared through the glass door into the dining hall.
Stragglers crossed, coming from the entrance, or the
lifts. Inside, they had already begun serving, but the
young Poles were still waiting around the little wicker
table; and Aschenbach, comfortably propped in his
deep chair, and with this beauty before his eyes, stayed
with them.

The governess, a small corpulent middle-class woman
with a red face, finally gave the sign to rise. With lifted
brows, she pushed back her chair and bowed, as a large
woman dressed in gray and richly jeweled with pearls
entered the lobby. This woman was advancing with
coolness and precision; her lightly powdered hair and
the lines of her dress were arranged with the simplicity
which always signifies taste in those quarters where
devoutness is taken as one element of dignity. She might
have been the wife of some high German official, except
that her jewelry added something fantastically lavish
to her appearance; indeed, it was almost priceless, and
consisted of ear pendants and a very long triple chain
of softly glowing pearls, as large as cherries.

The children had risen promptly. They bent over to kiss the hand of their mother, who, with a distant smile on her well-preserved though somewhat tired and peaked features, looked over their heads and directed a few words to the governess in French. Then she walked to the glass door. The children followed her: the girls in the order of their age, after them the governess, the boy last. For some reason or other he turned around before crossing the threshold, and since no one else was in the lobby his strange dusky eyes met those of Aschenbach, who, his newspaper on his knees, lost in thought, was gazing after the group.

What he saw had not been unusual in the slightest detail. They had not preceded the mother to the table; they had waited, greeted her with respect, and observed the customary forms on entering the room. But it had taken place so pointedly, with such an accent of training, duty, and self-respect, that Aschenbach felt peculiarly touched by it all. He delayed for a few moments, then he too crossed into the dining room, and was assigned to his table which, as he noted with a brief touch of regret, was very far removed from that of the Polish family.

Weary, and yet intellectually active, he entertained himself during the lengthy meal with abstract, or even transcendental things; he pondered on the dark alliance which must be contracted between universal law and the individually distinct for human beauty to result, from this he passed into general problems of form and art, and at the end he found that his thoughts and discoveries were like the seemingly felicitous promptings of a dream which, when the mind is sobered, are seen to be completely empty and unfit. After the meal, smoking, sitting, taking an occasional turn in the park with its

smell of nightfall, he went to bed early and spent the
night in a sleep deep and unbroken, but often enlivened
with the apparitions of dreams.

The weather did not improve any the following da . .
A land breeze was blowing. Under a cloudy ashen sky,
the sea lay in dull peacefulness; it seemed shriveled up,
with a close dreary horizon, and it had retreated from
the beach, baring the long ribs of several sandbanks.
As Aschenbach opened his window, he thought that he
could detect the foul smell of the lagoon.

He felt depressed. He thought already of leaving.
Once, years ago, after several weeks of spring here, this
same weather had afflicted him, and impaired his
health so seriously that he had to abandon Venice like
a fugitive. Was not this old feverish unrest again setting
in, the pressure in the temples, the heaviness of the
eyelids? It would be annoying to change his residence
still another time; but if the wind did not turn, he could
not stay here. To be safe, he did not unpack completely.
He breakfasted at nine in the buffet room provided for
this purpose between the lobby and the dining room.

That formal silence reigned here which is the ambition of large hotels. The waiters who were serving
walked about on soft soles. Nothing was audible but
the tinkling of the tea things, a word half whispered.
In one corner, obliquely across from the door, and two
tables removed from his own, Aschenbach observed the
Polish girls with their governess. Erect and red-eyed,
their ash-blond hair freshly smoothed down; dressed in
stiff blue linen with little white cuffs and turned-down
collars—they were sitting there, handing around a glass
of marmalade. They had almost finished their breakfast.
The boy was missing.

Aschenbach smiled. "Well, little Phaeacian!" he

thought. "You seem to be enjoying the pleasant privilege of having your sleep out." And, suddenly exhilarated, he recited to himself the line from The Odyssey:

A frequent change of dress; warm baths, and rest.

He breakfasted without haste. From the porter, who entered the hall holding his braided cap in his hand, he received some forwarded mail; and while he smoked a cigarette he opened a few letters. In this way it happened that he was present at the entrance of the late sleeper who was being waited for over yonder.

He came through the glass door and crossed the room in silence to his sisters' table. His approach—the way he held the upper part of his body, and bent his knees, the movement of his white-shod feet—had an extraordinary charm; he walked very lightly, at once timid and proud, and this became still more lovely through the childish embarrassment with which, twice as he proceeded, he turned his face toward the center of the room, raising and lowering his eyes. Smiling, with something half muttered in his soft vague tongue, he took his place; and now, as he turned his full profile to the observer, Aschenbach was again astonished, terrified even, by the really godlike beauty of this human child. Today the boy was wearing a light blouse of blue-and-white-striped cotton, with a red silk tie in front, and closed at the neck by a plain white high collar. This collar lacked the distinctiveness of the blouse, but above it the flowering head was poised with an incomparable seductiveness—the head of an Eros, in blended yellows of Parian marble, with fine serious brows, the temples and ears covered softly by the abrupt encroachment of his curls.

"Good, good!" Aschenbach thought, with that deliberate expert appraisal which artists sometimes employ as a subterfuge when they have been carried away with delight before a masterwork. And he thought further: "Really, if the sea and the beach weren't waiting for me, I should stay here as long as you stayed!" But he went then, passed through the lobby among the attentive servants, down the wide terrace, and straight across the boardwalk to the section of the beach reserved for the hotel guests. The barefoot old man in dungarees and straw hat who was functioning here as bathing master assigned him to the cabin he had rented; a table and a seat were placed on the sandy board platform, and he made himself comfortable in the lounge chair which he had drawn closer to the sea, out into the waxen yellow sand.

More than ever before, he was entertained and amused by the sights on the beach, this spectacle of carefree, civilized people getting sensuous enjoyment at the very edge of the elements. The gray flat sea was already alive with wading children, swimmers, a motley of figures lying on the sandbanks with arms bent behind their heads. Others were rowing about in little red-and-blue-striped boats without keels; they were continually upsetting, amid laughter. Before the long stretches of cabins, where people were sitting on the platforms as though on small verandas, there was a play of movement against the line of rest and inertness behind—visits and chatter, fastidious morning elegance alongside the nakedness which, boldly at ease, was enjoying the freedom which the place afforded. Farther in front, on the damp firm sand, people were parading about in white bathing cloaks, in ample, brilliantly colored wrappers. An elaborate sand pile to the right, erected by children, had flags in the colors of all nations planted around it. Venders of shells, cakes, and fruit spread out their wares, kneeling. To the left, before one of the cabins which stood at right angles to the others and to the sea, a Russian family was encamped: men with beards and large teeth, slow delicate women, a Baltic girl sitting by an easel and painting the sea amidst exclamations of despair, two ugly good-natured children, an old maidservant who wore a kerchief on her head and had the obsequious manners of an affectionate slave. Delighted and appreciative, they were busying themselves there, patiently calling the names of the two rowdy disobedient children, using their scanty Italian to joke with the humorous old man from whom they were buying candy, kissing one another on the cheek, and not in the least concerned with anyone who might be observing their community.

"Yes, I shall stay," Aschenbach thought. "Where would things be better?" And, his hands folded in his lap, he let his eyes lose themselves in the expanses of the sea, his gaze gliding, blurring, and failing in the monotone mist of the wilderness of space. He loved the ocean for deep-seated reasons: because of that yearning for rest, when the hard-pressed artist hungers to shut out the exacting multiplicities of experience and seek refuge on the breast of the simple, the vast; and because of a forbidden hankering—seductive, by virtue of its being directly opposed to his obligations—after the inarticulate, the boundless, the eternal, sheer nothing. To be at rest in the face of perfection is the hunger of everyone who is aiming at excellence; and what is nothingness if not a form of perfection? But now, just as his dreams had strayed so far into the void, suddenly the horizontal fringe of the sea was broken by a human figure; and as he brought his eyes back from the unbounded, and focused them, it was the lovely boy who was there, coming from the left and passing him on the sand. He was barefooted, ready for wading, his slender legs exposed above the knees; he walked slowly, but as lightly and proudly as though it were the customary thing for him to move about without shoes; and he was looking around him toward the line of cabins opposite. But as soon as he had noticed the Russian family, its members all getting along so well together, a cloud of scorn and detestation passed over his face. His brow darkened, his mouth was compressed, he gave his lips an embittered twist to one side, so that the cheek was distorted and the forehead became so heavily furrowed that the eyes seemed sunken beneath its pressure: malicious and glowering, they spoke the language of hate. He looked down, looked back once more threateningly, then with his shoulder made an abrupt gesture of disdain and dismissal, and left the enemy behind him.

A kind of pudency or confusion, something like respect and shyness, caused Aschenbach to turn away as though he had seen nothing. For the earnest-minded who have been casual observers of some passion, struggle against making use, even to themselves, of what they have seen. But he was both cheered and shaken —which is to say, he was happy. This childish fanaticism, directed against the most good-natured possible aspect of life—it brought the divinely arbitrary into human relationships; it made a delightful natural picture which had appealed only to the eye now seem worthy of a deeper sympathy; and it gave the figure of this half-grown boy, who had already been notable enough by his sheer beauty, something to offset him still further, and to make one take him more seriously than his years justified. Still looking away, Aschenbach could hear the boy's voice, the clear, somewhat weak voice with which, in the distance now, he was trying to call hello to his playfellows busied around the sand pile. They answered him, shouting back his name, or some affectionate nickname; and Aschenbach listened with a certain curiosity, without being able to catch anything more definite than two melodic syllables like "Adgio," or still more frequently "Adgiu," with a ringing *u*-sound prolonged at the end. He was pleased with the resonance of this; he found it adequate to the subject. He repeated it silently and, satisfied, turned to his letters and manuscripts.

His small traveling-pad on his knees, he began writing with his fountain pen an answer to this or that bit of correspondence. But after the first fifteen minutes he found it a pity to misuse the occasion—the most enjoyable he could think of—in this manner and miss it in indifferent activities which did not interest him. He tossed the writing materials to one side, and he faced the ocean again; soon afterward, diverted by the childish voices around the sand heap, he revolved his head comfortably along the back of the chair toward the right, to discover where that excellent little Adgio might be and what he was doing.

He was found at a glance; the red tie on his breast was not to be overlooked. Busied with the others in laying an old plank across the damp moat of the sand castle, he was nodding, and shouting instructions for this work. There were about ten companions with him, boys and girls of his age, and a few younger ones who were chattering with one another in Polish, French, and several Balkan tongues. But it was his name which rang out most often. He was obviously in demand, sought after, admired. One boy especially, like him a Pole, a stocky fellow who was called something like "Jaschu," with sleek black hair and a belted linen coat, seemed to be his closest vassal and friend. When the work on the sand structure was finished for the time being, they walked arm in arm along the beach, and the boy who was called "Jaschu" kissed the beauty.

Aschenbach was half minded to raise a warning finger. "I advise you, Critobulus," he thought, smiling, "to travel for a year! For you need that much time at least to get over it." And then he breakfasted on large ripe strawberries which he got from a peddler. It had become very warm, although the sun could not penetrate the blanket of mist in the sky. Laziness clogged his brain, even while his senses delighted in the numbing, drugging distractions of the ocean's stillness. To guess, to puzzle out just what name it was that sounded something like "Adgio," seemed to the sober man an appropriate ambition, a thoroughly engrossing pursuit. And with the aid of a few scrappy recollections of Polish he decided that it must be "Tadzio," the shortened form of "Tadeusz," and sounding in the vocative like "Tadziu."

Tadzio was bathing. Aschenbach, who had lost sight of him, spied his head and the arm with which he was propelling himself, far out in the water; for the sea must have been smooth for a long distance out. But already people seemed worried about him; women's voices were calling after him from the cabins, uttering this name again and again. It almost dominated the beach like a battle cry, and with its soft consonants, its long-drawn *u*-note at the end, it had something at once sweet and wild about it: "Tadziu! Tadziu!" He turned back; beating the resistant water into a foam with his legs, he hurried, his head bent down over the waves. And to see how this vital figure, virginally graceful and unripe, with dripping curls, and lovely as some slender god, came up out of the depths of sky and sea, rose and separated from the elements—this spectacle aroused a sense of myth, it was like some poet's recovery of time at its beginning, of the origin of forms and the birth of gods. Aschenbach listened with closed eyes to this song ringing within him, and he thought again that it was pleasant here, and that he would like to remain.

Later Tadzio was resting from his bath; he lay in the sand, wrapped in his white robe, which was drawn under the right shoulder, his head supported on his bare arm. And even when Aschenbach was not observing him, but was reading a few pages in his book, he hardly ever forgot that this boy was lying there and that it would cost him only a slight turn of his head to the right to behold the marvel. It seemed that he was sitting here just to keep watch over the youth's repose—busied with his own concerns, and yet constantly aware of this noble picture at his right, not far in the distance. And he was stirred by a paternal affection, the profound leaning which those who have devoted their thoughts to the creation of beauty feel toward those who possess beauty itself.

A little past noon he left the beach, returned to the hotel, and was taken up to his room. He stayed there for some time in front of the mirror, looking at his gray hair, his tired sharp features. At this moment he thought of his reputation, and of the fact that he was often recognized on the streets and observed with respect, thanks to the sure aim and the appealing finish of his words. He called up all the exterior successes of his talent which he could think of, remembering also his elevation to the knighthood. Then he went down to the dining hall for lunch, and ate at his little table. As he was riding up in the lift, after the meal was ended, a group of young people also coming from lunch pressed into the swaying cage after him, and Tadzio entered too. He stood quite near to Aschenbach, for the first time so near that Aschenbach could see him, not with the aloofness of a picture, but in minute detail, in all his human particularities. The boy was addressed by someone or other, and as he was answering with an indescribably agreeable smile he stepped out again, on the second floor, walking backward, and with his eyes lowered. "Beauty makes modest," Aschenbach thought, and he tried insistently to explain why this was so. But he had noticed that Tadzio's teeth were not all they should be; they were somewhat jagged and pale. The enamel did not look healthy; it had a peculiar brittleness and transparency, as is often the case with anemics. "He is very frail, he is sickly," Aschenbach thought. "In all probability he will not grow old." And he refused to reckon with the feeling of gratification or reassurance which accompanied this notion.

He spent two hours in his room, and in the afternoon he rode in the *vaporetto* across the foul-smelling lagoon to Venice. He got off at San Marco, took tea on the Piazza, and then, in accord with his daily schedule here, he went for a walk through the streets. Yet it was this walk which produced a complete reversal in his attitudes and his plans.

An offensive sultriness lay over the streets. The air

was so heavy that the smells pouring out of homes, stores, and eating houses became mixed with oil, vapors, clouds of perfumes, and still other odors—and these would not blow away, but hung in layers. Cigarette smoke remained suspended, disappearing very slowly. The crush of people along the narrow streets irritated rather than entertained the walker. The farther he went, the more he was depressed by the repulsive condition resulting from the combination of sea air and sirocco, which was at the same time both stimulating and enervating. He broke into an uncomfortable sweat. His eyes failed him, his chest became tight, he felt feverish, the blood was pounding in his head. He fled from the crowded business streets across bridges into the walks of the poor. On a quiet square, one of those forgotten and enchanting places which lie in the interior of Venice, he rested at the brink of a well, dried his forehead, and realized that he would have to leave here.

For the second time, and now quite definitely, it had been demonstrated that this city in this kind of weather was decidedly unhealthy for him. It seemed foolish to attempt a stubborn resistance, while the prospects for a change of wind were completely uncertain. A quick decision was called for. It was not possible to go home this soon. Neither summer nor winter quarters were prepared to receive him. But this was not the only place where there were sea and beach; and elsewhere these could be found without the lagoon and its malarial fumes. He remembered a little watering place not far from Trieste which had been praised to him. Why not there? And without delay, so that this new change of location would still have time to do him some good. He pronounced this as good as settled, and stood up.

At the next gondola station he took a boat back to San Marco, and was led through the dreary labyrinth of canals, under fancy marble balconies flanked with lions, around the corners of smooth walls, past the sorrowing façade of palaces which mirrored large dilapidated business signs in the pulsing water. He had trouble arriving there, for the gondolier, who was in league with lace-makers and glass-blowers, was always trying to land him for inspections and purchases; and just as the bizarre trip through Venice would begin to cast its spell, the greedy business sense of the sunken Queen did all it could to destroy the illusion.

When he had returned to the hotel, he announced at the office before dinner that unforeseen developments necessitated his departure the following morning. He was assured of their regrets. He settled his accounts. He dined, and spent the warm evening reading the newspapers in a rocking chair on the rear terrace. Before going to bed he got his luggage all ready for departure.

He did not sleep so well as he might, since the impending break-up made him restless. When he opened the window in the morning, the sky was as overcast as ever, but the air seemed fresher, and he was already beginning to repent. Hadn't his decision been somewhat hasty and uncalled for, the result of a passing diffidence and indisposition? If he had delayed a little, if, instead of surrendering so easily, he had made some attempt to adjust himself to the air of Venice or to wait for an improvement in the weather, he would not be so rushed and inconvenienced, but could anticipate another forenoon on the beach like yesterday's. Too late. Now he would have to go on wanting what he had wanted yesterday. He dressed, and at about eight o'clock rode down to the ground floor for breakfast.

As he entered, the breakfast room was still empty of guests. A few came in while he sat waiting for his order. With his teacup to his lips, he saw the Polish girls and their governess appear: rigid, with morning freshness, their eyes still red, they walked across to their table in the corner by the window. Immediately afterward, the porter approached him, cap in hand, and warned him that it was time to go. The automobile is ready to take him and the other passengers to the Hotel Excelsior, and from here the motorboat will bring the ladies and gentlemen to the station through the company's private canal. Time is pressing. Aschenbach found that it was doing nothing of the sort. It was still over an hour before his train left. He was irritated by this hotel custom of hustling departing guests out of the house, and indicated to the porter that he wished to finish his breakfast in peace. The man retired hesitatingly, to appear again five minutes later. It is impossible for the car to wait any longer. Then he would take a cab, and carry his trunk with him, Aschenbach replied in anger. He would use the public steamboat at the proper time, and he requested that it be left to him personally to worry about his departure. The employee bowed himself away. Pleased with the way he had warded off these importunate warnings, Aschenbach finished his meal at leisure; in fact, he even had the waiter bring him a newspaper. The time had become quite short when he finally arose. It so happened that at the same moment Tadzio should come through the glass door.

On the way to his table he crossed the path of the departing guest; he lowered his eyes modestly before the

man with the gray hair and high forehead, only to raise
them again, in his delicious manner, soft and full upon
him—and he had passed. "Good-bye, Tadzio!" Aschenbach thought. "I did not see you for long." He did what
was unusual with him, really formed the words on his
lips and spoke them to himself; then he added: "God
bless you!" After this he left, distributed tips, was
ushered out by the small gentle manager in the French
frock coat, and made off from the hotel on foot, as he
had come, going along the white-blossoming avenue
which crossed the island to the steamer bridge, accompanied by the house servant carrying his hand luggage.
He arrived, took his place—and then there followed a
painful journey through all the depths of regret.

It was the familiar trip across the lagoon, past San
Marco, up the Grand Canal. Aschenbach sat on the circular bench at the bow, his arm supported against the
railing, shading his eyes with his hand. The public
gardens were left behind, the Piazzetta opened up once
more in princely splendor and was gone, then came the
great flock of palaces, and as the channel made a turn
the magnificently slung marble arch of the Rialto came
into view. The traveler was watching; his emotions were
in conflict. The atmosphere of the city, this slightly
foul smell of sea and swamp which he had been so anxious to avoid—he breathed it now in deep, exquisitely
painful draughts. Was it possible that he had not
known, had not considered, just how much he was at-
tached to all this? What had been a partial misgiving
this morning, a faint doubt as to the advisability of his
move, now became a distress, a positive misery, a spiritual hunger, and so bitter that it frequently brought
tears to his eyes, while he told himself that he could not

possibly have foreseen it. Hardest of all to bear, at times completely insufferable, was the thought that he would never see Venice again, that this was a leave-taking forever. Since it had been shown for the second time that the city affected his health, since he was compelled for the second time to get away in all haste, from now on he would have to consider it a place impossible and forbidden to him, a place which he was not equal to, and which it would be foolish for him to visit again. Yes, he felt that if he left now, wounded pride would prevent him from ever seeing again the beloved city where he had twice failed physically. And of a sudden this struggle between his desires and his physical strength seemed to the aging man so grave and important, his physical defeat seemed so dishonorable, so much a challenge to hold out at any cost, that he could not understand the ready submissiveness of the day before, when he had decided to give in without attempting any serious resistance.

Meanwhile the steamboat was nearing the station; pain and perplexity increased, he became distracted. In his affliction, he felt that it was impossible to leave, and just as impossible to turn back. The conflict was intense as he entered the station. It was very late; there was not a moment to lose if he was to catch the train. He wanted to, and he did not want to. But time was pressing; it drove him on. He hurried to get his ticket, and looked about in the tumult of the hall for the officer on duty here from the hotel. The man appeared and announced that the large trunk had already gone. Gone already? Yes—we can assure you—to Como. To Como! And after much checking back and forth, amidst angry questions and muddled answers, it came to light that the trunk had already been sent, with the baggage of other guests, from the express office of the Hotel Excelsior in a completely wrong direction.

Aschenbach had difficulty in preserving the expression which was required under these circumstances. He was almost convulsed with an adventurous delight, an unbelievable hilarity. The employee rushed off to see if it were still possible to stop the trunk, and, as was to be expected, he returned with nothing accomplished. Aschenbach declared that he did not want to travel without his trunk, but had decided to go back and wait at the Beach Hotel for its return. Was the company's motorboat still at the station? The man assured him that it was lying at the door. With Italian volubility he persuaded the clerk at the ticket window to take back the ticket already bought, he swore that they would act speedily, that no time or money would be spared in recovering the trunk promptly, and—so the strange thing happened that, twenty minutes after his arrival at the station, the traveler found himself again on the Grand Canal, returning to the Lido.

Here was an adventure, wonderful, abashing, and comically dreamlike beyond belief: places which he had just bid farewell to forever in the most abject misery— yet he had been turned and driven back by fate, and was seeing them again in the same hour! The spray from the prow, washing between gondolas and steamers with an absurd agility, shot the speedy little craft ahead to its goal, while the lone passenger was hiding the nervousness and ebullience of a truant boy under a mask of resigned anger. From time to time he shook with laughter at this mishap which, as he told himself, could not have turned out more luckily. There were explanations to be given, expressions of astonishment to be faced—and then, he told himself, everything would be all right; then a misfortune would have been avoided, a grave error rectified. And all that he had thought he was leaving behind him would be open to him again, there at his disposal. . . . And, to cap it all, was the rapidity of the ride deceiving him, or was the wind really coming from the sea?

The waves beat against the walls of the narrow canal which runs through the island to the Hotel Excelsior. An automobile omnibus was awaiting his return there, and took him above the rippling sea straight to the Beach Hotel. The little manager with mustache and long-tailed frock coat came down the stairs to meet him.

He ingratiatingly regretted the episode, spoke of it as highly painful to him and the establishment, but firmly approved of Aschenbach's decision to wait here for the baggage. Of course his room had been given up, but there was another one, just as good, which he could occupy immediately. "*Pas de chance, monsieur,*" the Swiss elevator boy smiled as they were ascending. And so the fugitive was established again, in a room almost identical with the other in its location and furnishings.

Tired out by the confusion of this strange forenoon, he distributed the contents of his hand bag about the room and dropped into an armchair by the open window. The sea had become a pale green, the air seemed thinner and purer; the beach, with its cabins and boats, seemed to have color, although the sky was still gray. Aschenbach looked out, his hands folded in his lap; he was content to be back, but shook his head disapprovingly at his irresolution, his failure to know his own mind. He sat here for the better part of an hour, resting

and dreaming vaguely. About noon he saw Tadzio in a
striped linen suit with a red tie, coming back from the
sea across the private beach and along the boardwalk
to the hotel. Aschenbach recognized him from this alti-
tude before he had actually set eyes on him; he was
about to think some such words as "Well, Tadzio, there
you are again!" but at the same moment he felt this
careless greeting go dumb before the truth in his heart.
He felt the exhilaration of his blood, a conflict of pain
and pleasure, and he realized that it was Tadzio who
had made it so difficult for him to leave.

He sat very still, entirely unobserved from this
height, and looked within himself. His features were
alert, his eyebrows raised, and an attentive, keenly
inquisitive smile distended his mouth. Then he raised
his head, lifted both hands, which had hung relaxed
over the arms of the chair, and in a slow twisting movement turned the palms upward—as though to suggest
an opening and spreading outward of his arms. It was a
spontaneous gesture of welcome, of calm acceptance.

I V

DAY after day now the naked god with the hot cheeks
drove his fire-breathing quadriga across the expanses of
the sky, and his yellow locks fluttered in the assault of
the east wind. A white silk sheen stretched over the

slowly simmering Ponto. The sand glowed. Beneath the quaking silver blue of the ether, rust-colored canvases were spread in front of the cabins, and the afternoons were spent in the sharply demarcated spots of shade which they cast. But it was also delightful in the evening, when the vegetation in the park had the smell of balsam, and the stars were working through their courses above, and the soft persistent murmur of the sea came up enchantingly through the night. Such evenings contained the cheering promise that more sunny days of casual idleness would follow, dotted with countless closely interspersed possibilities of well-timed accidents.

The guest who was detained here by such an accommodating mishap did not consider the return of his property as sufficient grounds for another departure. He suffered some inconvenience for two days, and had to appear for meals in the large dining room in his traveling clothes. When the strayed luggage was finally deposited in his room again, he unpacked completely and filled the closet and drawers with his belongings; he had decided to remain here indefinitely, content now that he could pass the hours on the beach in a silk suit and appear for dinner at his little table again in appropriate evening dress.

The comfortable rhythm of this life had already cast its spell over him; he was soon enticed by the ease, the mild splendor, of his program. Indeed, what a place to be in, when the charms of good living in a seaside resort on a southern shore were coupled with the immediate nearness of the most wonderful of all cities! Aschenbach was not a lover of pleasure. Whenever there was some call for him to take a holiday, to indulge himself, to have a good time—and this was especially true at an earlier age—restlessness and repugnance soon drove him back to his rigorous toil, the faithful sober efforts of his daily routine. But this place was bewitching him, relaxing his will, making him happy. In the mornings, under the shelter of his cabin, letting his eyes roam dreamily in the blue of the southern sea; or on a warm night as he leaned back against the cushions of the gondola carrying him under the broad starry sky home to the Lido from the Piazza di San Marco after long hours of idleness—and the brilliant lights, the melting notes of the serenade were being left behind—he would recall his place in the mountains, the scene of his battles in the summer, where the clouds blew low across his garden, and terrifying storms put out the lamps at night, and the crows which he fed were swinging in the tops of the pine trees. Then it would seem to him as though he were lifted into the Elysian fields, on the borders of the earth, where man enjoys the easiest life, where there is no snow or winter, nor storms and pouring rains, but where Oceanus continually sènds forth gentle cooling breezes, and the days pass in a blessed inactivity, without work, without effort, devoted wholly to the sun and to the feast days of the sun.

Aschenbach saw young Tadzio frequently, almost constantly. Owing to the limited range of territory and the regularity of their lives, the beauty was near him at short intervals throughout the day. He saw him, met him, everywhere: in the lower rooms of the hotel, on the cooling water trips to the city and back, in the splendor of the square, and at times when he was especially lucky ran across him on the streets. But princi-

pally, and with the most gratifying regularity, the forenoon on the beach allowed him to admire and study
this rare spectacle at his leisure. Yes, it was this guar-
anty of happiness, this daily recurrence of good fortune,
which made his stay here so precious, and gave him
such pleasure in the constant procession of sunny days.

He was up as early as he used to be when under the
driving pressure of work, and was on the beach before
most people, when the sun was still mild and the sea
lay blinding white in the dreaminess of morning. He
spoke amiably to the guard of the private beach, and
also spoke familiarly to the barefoot, white-bearded old
man who had prepared his place for him, stretching the
brown canopy and bringing the furniture of the cabin
out on the platform. Then he took his seat. There would
now be three or four hours in which the sun mounted
and gained terrific strength, the sea a deeper and deeper
blue, and he might look at Tadzio.

He saw him approaching from the left, along the edge
of the sea; he saw him as he stepped out backward from
among the cabins; or he would suddenly find, with a
shock of pleasure, that he had missed his coming, that
he was already here in the blue-and-white bathing suit
which was his only garment now while on the beach,
that he had already commenced his usual activities in
the sun and the sand—a pleasantly trifling, idle, and
unstable manner of living, a mixture of rest and play.
Tadzio would saunter about, wade, dig, catch things,
lie down, go for a swim, all the while being kept under
surveillance by the women on the platform who made
his name ring out in their falsetto voices: "Tadziu!
Tadziu!" Then he would come running to them with a
look of eagerness, to tell them what he had seen, what he

had experienced, or to show them what he had found or caught: mussels, sea horses, jellyfish, and crabs that ran sideways. Aschenbach did not understand a word he said, and though it might have been the most ordinary thing in the world, it was a vague harmony in his ear. So the foreignness of the boy's speech turned it into music, a wanton sun poured its prodigal splendor down over him, and his figure was always set off against the background of an intense sea blue.

This buoyant body bore itself so freely that his eyes soon knew every line and posture. He was continually rediscovering with new pleasure all this familiar beauty, and his astonishment at its delicate appeal to his senses was unending. The boy was called to greet a guest who was paying his respects to the ladies at their cabin. He came running, running wet perhaps out of the water, tossed back his curls, and as he held out his hand, resting on one leg and raising his other foot on the toes, the set of his body was delightful; it had a charming expectancy about it, a lovely shyness, a winsomeness which showed the effect of his breeding. . . . He lay stretched full-length, his bath towel slung across his shoulders, his delicately chiseled arm supported in the sand, his chin in his palm; the boy called Jaschu was squatting near him and making up to him—and nothing could be more enchanting than the smile of his eyes and lips when, in his eminence, he glanced up at his inferior, his servant. . . . He stood on the edge of the sea, alone, apart from his people, quite near to Aschenbach—erect, his hands locked across the back of his neck, he swayed slowly on the balls of his feet, looked dreamily into the blueness of sea and sky, while tiny waves rolled up and bathed his feet. His honey-colored hair clung in rings about his neck and temples. The sun made the down on his back glitter; the fine etching of the ribs, the symmetry of the chest, showed through the flesh thinly covering his torso. His armpits were still as smooth as those of a statue; the hollows of his knees glistened, and their bluish veins made his body seem built of some clearer stuff. What rigor, what precision of thought were expressed in this erect, youthfully perfect body! Yet the pure and strenuous will which, darkly at work, could bring such godlike sculpture to the light—was not he, the artist, at home with this? Was it not working in him too when, under the pressure of an abstemious passion, he would free from the marble mass of speech some slender form which he had seen in the mind and which he put before his fellows as a statue and a mirror of intellectual beauty?

Statue and mirror! His eyes took in the noble form there bordered with blue; and with a rush of enthusiasm he felt that in this spectacle he was grasping the very essence of beauty, form as the thought of God, the one pure perfection which lives in the mind, and which, in this symbol and likeness, had been placed here quietly and simply as an object of devotion. That was drunkenness; and eagerly, without thinking, the aging artist welcomed it. His mind was in travail; all that he had learned dropped back into flux; his understanding threw up age-old thoughts which he had inherited with youth though they had never before lived with their own fire. Is it not written that the sun diverts our attention from intellectual to sensual things? Reason and understanding, it is said, become so numbed and enchanted that the soul forgets everything out of delight with its immediate circumstances, and in astonishment becomes at-

tached to the most beautiful object shined on by the
sun; indeed, only with the aid of a body is it capable
then of raising itself to thoughts of a higher order. In
truth, Amor did as mathematicians who show uncom-
prehending children tangible representations of pure
forms—similarly, in order to make the spiritual visible
for us, the god availed himself of the figure and color of
human youth; and as a reminder he adorned these with
the reflected splendor of beauty which, when we behold
it, makes us flare up in pain and hope.

His enthusiasm suggested these things, put him in
the mood for them. And from the sound of the sea and
the luster of the sun he wove himself a charming picture.
Here was the old plane tree, not far from the walls of
Athens—a holy, shadowy place filled with the smell of
agnus castus blossoms and decorated with ornaments
and images sacred to Achelous and the Nymphs. Clear
and pure, the brook at the foot of the spreading tree
fell across the smooth pebbles; the cicadas were fiddling.
But on the grass, which was like a pillow gently sloping
to the head, two people were stretched out, in hiding
from the heat of the day: an older man and a youth, one
ugly and one beautiful, wisdom next to loveliness.
And amid gallantries and brightly engaging banter,
Socrates was instructing Phaedrus in matters of desire
and virtue. He spoke to him of the hot terror which the
initiates suffer when their eyes light on an image of the
eternal beauty; spoke of the greed of the impious and
the wicked who cannot think beauty when they see its
likeness, and who are incapable of reverence; spoke of
the holy distress which befalls the noble-minded when a
godlike countenance, a perfect body, appears before
them; they tremble and grow distracted, and hardly

dare to raise their eyes, and they honor the man who possesses this beauty, yes, if they were not afraid of being thought downright madmen they would sacrifice to the beloved as to the image of a god. For beauty, my Phaedrus, beauty alone is both lovely and visible at once; it is, mark me, the only form of the spiritual which we can receive through the senses. Else what would become of us if the divine, if reason and virtue and truth, should appear to us through the senses? Should we not perish and be consumed with love, as Semele once was with Zeus? Thus, beauty is the sensitive man's access to the spirit—but only a road, a means simply, little Phaedrus. . . . And then this crafty suitor made the neatest remark of all; it was this, that the lover is more divine than the beloved, since the god is in the one, but not in the other—perhaps the most delicate, the most derisive thought which has ever been framed, and the one from which spring all the cunning and the profoundest pleasures of desire.

Writers are happiest with an idea which can become all emotion, and an emotion all idea. Just such a pulsating idea, such a precise emotion, belonged to the lonely man at this moment, was at his call. Nature, it ran, shivers with ecstasy when the spirit bows in homage before beauty. Suddenly he wanted to write. Eros loves idleness, they say, and he is suited only to idleness. But at this point in the crisis the affliction became a stimulus toward productivity. The incentive hardly mattered. An inquiry, a request for an open statement on a certain large burning issue of culture and taste, was being circulated in the intellectual world, and had finally caught up with the traveler here. He was familiar with the subject, it had touched his own experience; and suddenly he felt an irresistible desire to illuminate it in the light of his particular terms. Moreover, he would do the work in Tadzio's presence, taking the figure of the boy as a standard for his writing, making his style follow the lines of this body which seemed godlike to him, and carrying his beauty over into the spiritual just as the eagle once carried the Trojan shepherd up into the ether. Never had his joy in words been more sweet. He had never been so aware that Eros is in the word as during those perilously precious hours when, at his crude table under the canopy, facing the idol and listening to the music of his voice, he followed Tadzio's beauty in the forming of his little tract, a page and a half of choice prose which was soon to kindle the acclaim of many through its clarity, its poise, and its vibrant emotional tension. Certainly it is better for people to know the beautiful product only as finished, and not in its conception, its conditions of origin. For knowledge of the sources from which the artist derives his inspiration would often confuse and alienate, and in this way detract from the effects of his mastery. Strange hours! Strangely enervating efforts! Rare creative intercourse between the spirit and body! When Aschenbach put away his work and started back from the beach, he felt exhausted, or even deranged; and it seemed that his conscience was rebuking him, as if after a debauch.

The following morning, as he was about to leave the hotel, he looked off from the steps and noticed that Tadzio, who was alone and was already on his way toward the sea, was just approaching the private beach. He was half tempted by the simple notion of seizing this opportunity to strike up a casual friendly acquaintanceship with the boy who had unknowingly evoked in him such agitation and exaltation; he wanted to address him, and enjoy the answering look in his eyes. The boy was sauntering along, he could be overtaken; and Aschenbach quickened his pace. He reached him on the boardwalk behind the cabins; was about to lay a hand on his head and shoulders; and some word or other, an amiable phrase in French, was on the tip of his tongue. But he felt that his heart, perhaps also because of his rapid stride, was beating like a hammer; and he was so short of breath that his voice would have been tight and trembling. He hesitated, he tried to get himself under control. Suddenly he became afraid that he had been walking too long so close behind the boy. He was afraid of arousing his curiosity and causing him to look back questioningly. He made one more spurt, failed, surrendered, and passed with bowed head.

"Too late!" he thought immediately. "Too late!" Yet was it too late? This step which he had just been on the verge of taking would very possibly have put things on a sound, free and easy basis, and would have restored him to wholesome soberness. But the fact was that Aschenbach did not want soberness: his intoxication was too precious. Who can explain the stamp and the nature of the artist? Who can understand this deep instinctive welding of discipline and license? For to be unable to want wholesome soberness is license. Aschenbach was no longer given to self-criticism. His tastes, the mental caliber of his years, his self-respect, ripeness, and a belated simplicity made him unwilling to dismember his motives and to debate whether it was his conscience or, on the contrary, dissoluteness and weakness, that had prevented him from carrying out his plans. He was embarrassed, as he feared that someone or other, if only the guard on the beach, must have observed his pursuit and defeat. He was very much afraid of the ridiculous. Further, he joked with himself about his comically pious distress. "Downed," he thought, "downed like a rooster, with his wings hanging miserably in the battle. It really is a god who, at the sight of loveliness, can undo our courage and lay low our pride so thoroughly. . . ." He toyed and skirmished with his emotions, and was far too haughty to be afraid of them.

He had already ceased thinking about the time when the vacation which he had allowed for would expire; the thought of going home never even suggested itself. He had sent for an ample supply of money. His only concern was with the possible departure of the Polish family; but by a casual questioning of the hotel barber he had contrived to learn that these people had come here only a short time before his own arrival. The sun browned his face and hands, the invigorating salt breezes made him feel more keenly. Once he had been in the habit of expending on his work every bit of energy that food, sleep, or nature could provide him; but now he was grandly spendthrift, letting pass off as elation and emotion all the strength daily derived from the sun, idleness, and sea air.

His sleep was fitful; the preciously uniform days were separated by short nights of happy unrest. He did retire early, for at nine o'clock, when Tadzio had disappeared from the scene, the day seemed over. But at the first gray of dawn he was awakened by a gently insistent shock; he suddenly remembered his adventure, he could no longer remain in bed; he arose and, clad lightly against the chill of morning, he sat down by the open window to await the rising of the sun. Toned by his sleep, he watched this miraculous event with reverence. Sky, earth, and sea still lay in glassy, ghostlike twilight; a dying star still floated in the emptiness of space. But a breeze started up, a winged message from habitations beyond reach, telling that Eos was rising from beside her husband. And that first sweet reddening in the farthest stretches of sky and sea took place by which the sentiency of creation is announced. The goddess was approaching, the seductress of youth who stole Cleitus and Cephalus, and despite the envy of all the Olympians enjoyed the love of handsome Orion. A strewing of roses began there on the edge of the world, an unutterably pure glowing and blooming. Tiny clouds, illumined and translucent, floated like busy little Cupids in the rosy, bluish mist. Purple fell upon the sea, which seemed to be simmering, and washing the color toward him. Golden spears shot up into the sky from below. The splendor caught fire, silently; with godlike power an intense flame of licking tongues broke out—and with rattling hoofs the brother's sacred chargers mounted the horizon. Lighted by the god's brilliance, he sat there, keeping watch alone. He closed his eyes, letting this glory play against the lids. Past emotions, precious early afflictions and yearnings which had been stifled by his rigorous program of living, were now returning in such strange new forms. With an embarrassed, astonished smile, he recognized them. He was thinking, dreaming; slowly his lips formed a name. And still smiling, with his face turned upward, hands folded in his lap, he fell asleep again in his chair.

But the day which began with such fiery solemnity underwent a strange mythical transformation. Where did the breeze originate which suddenly began playing so gently and insinuatingly, like some whispered suggestion, about his ears and temples? Little white choppy clouds stood in the sky in scattered clumps, like the pasturing herds of the gods. A stronger wind arose, and the steeds of Poseidon came prancing up, and along with them the steers which belonged to the blue-locked god, bellowing and lowering their horns as they ran. Yet among the crags of the more distant beach, waves were hopping forward like agile goats. He was caught in the enchantment of a sacredly distorted world full of Panic life—and he dreamed delicate legends. Often, when the sun was sinking behind Venice, he would sit on a bench in the park observing Tadzio, who was dressed in a white suit with a colored sash and was playing ball on the smooth gravel—and it was Hyacinth that he seemed to be watching, Hyacinth who was to die because two gods loved him. Yes, he felt Zephyr's aching jealousy of the rival who forgot the oracle, the bow, and the lyre, in order to play forever with this beauty. He saw the discus, guided by a pitiless envy, strike the lovely head; he too, growing pale, caught the drooping body—and the flower, sprung from this sweet blood, bore the inscription of his unending grief.

Nothing is stranger and more delicate than the relationship between people who know each other only with their eyes, who meet daily, even hourly, and yet are compelled, by force of custom or their own caprices, to say no word or make no move of acknowledgment, but to maintain the appearance of an aloof unconcern. There is a restlessness and a surcharged curiosity existing between them, the hysteria of an unsatisfied, unnaturally repressed desire for acquaintanceship and interchange; and especially there is a kind of tense respect. For one person loves and honors another so long as he cannot judge him, and desire is a product of incomplete knowledge.

Some kind of familiarity had necessarily to form itself between Aschenbach and young Tadzio; and it gave the elderly man keen pleasure to see that his sympathies and interests were not left completely unanswered. For example, when the boy appeared on the beach in the morning and was going toward his family's cabin, what had induced him never to use the boardwalk on the far side of it any more, but to stroll along the front path, through the sand, past Aschenbach's habitual place, and often unnecessarily close to him, almost touching his table, or his chair even? Did the attraction, the fascination of an overpowering emotion, have such an effect upon the frail unthinking object of it? Aschenbach watched daily for Tadzio to approach; and sometimes he acted as though he were occupied when this event was taking place, and he let the boy pass seemingly unobserved. But at other times he would look up, and their glances met. They were both in deep earnest when this occurred. Nothing in the elderly man's cultivated and dignified expression betrayed any inner movement; but there was a searching look in Tadzio's eyes, a thoughtful questioning—he began to falter, looked down, then looked up again charmingly, and, when he had passed, something in his bearing seemed to indicate that it was only his breeding which kept him from turning around.

Once, however, one evening, things turned out differently. The Polish children and their governess had been missing at dinner in the large hall; Aschenbach had noted this uneasily. After the meal, disturbed by their absence, Aschenbach was walking in evening dress and straw hat in front of the hotel at the foot of the terrace, when suddenly he saw the nunlike sisters appear in the light of the arc lamp, accompanied by their governess and with Tadzio a few steps behind. Evidently they were coming from the steamer pier after having dined for some reason in the city. It must have been cool on the water; Tadzio was wearing a dark blue sailor overcoat with gold buttons, and on his head he had a cap to match. The sun and sea air had not browned him; his skin still had the same yellow marble color as at first. It even seemed paler today than usual, whether from the coolness or from the blanching moonlight of the lamps. His shapely eyebrows showed up more clearly, the darkness of his eyes was deeper. It is hard to say how beautiful he was; and Aschenbach was distressed, as he had often been before, by the thought that words can but praise sensuous beauty, not match it.

He had not been prepared for this precious spectacle; it came unhoped for. He had no time to entrench himself behind an expression of repose and dignity. Pleasure, surprise, admiration must have shown on his face as his eyes met those of the boy—and at this moment it happened that Tadzio smiled, smiled to him, eloquently, familiarly, charmingly, without concealment; and during the smile his lips slowly opened. It was the smile of Narcissus bent over the reflecting water, that deep, fascinated, magnetic smile with which he stretches out his arms to the image of his own beauty—a smile distorted ever so little, distorted at the hopelessness of his efforts to kiss the pure lips of the shadow. It was coquettish, inquisitive, and slightly tortured. It was infatuated, and infatuating.

He had received this smile, and he hurried away as though he bore a fatal gift. He was so shaken that he had to flee the light of the terrace and the front garden; he hastily hunted out the darkness of the park in the rear. Strangely indignant and tender admonitions wrung themselves out of him: "You dare not smile like that! Listen, no one dare smile like that to another!" He threw himself down on a bench; in a frenzy he breathed the night smell of the vegetation. And leaning back, his arms loose, overwhelmed, with shivers running through him, he whispered the fixed formula of desire —impossible in this case, absurd, abject, ridiculous, and yet holy, even in this case venerable: "I love you!"

V

DURING his fourth week at the Lido, Gustav von Aschenbach made several sinister observations touching on the world about him. First, it seemed to him that as the season progressed the number of guests at the hotel was diminishing rather than increasing; and German especially seemed to be dropping away, so that finally he heard nothing but foreign sounds at table and on the beach. Then one day in conversation with the barber, whom he visited often, he caught a word which startled him. The man had mentioned a German family that left soon after their arrival; he added glibly and flatteringly: "But you are staying, sir. You have no fear of the plague." Aschenbach looked at him. "The plague?" he repeated. The gossiper was silent, made out as though busy with other things, ignored the question. When it was put more insistently, he declared that he knew nothing, and with embarrassed volubility he tried to change the subject.

That was about noon. In the afternoon there was a calm, and Aschenbach rode to Venice under an intense sun. For he was driven by a mania to follow the Polish children, whom he had seen with their governess taking the road to the steamer pier. He did not find the idol at San Marco. But while sitting over his tea at his little round iron table on the shady side of the square, he suddenly detected a peculiar odor in the air which, it seemed to him now, he had sensed for days without being consciously aware of it. The smell was sweetish and druglike, suggesting sickness, and wounds, and a suspicious cleanliness. After thoughtful examination, he recognized it, finished his tea, and left the square on the side opposite the church. The smell was stronger where the street narrowed. On the corners printed posters were hung, giving municipal warnings against certain diseases of the gastric system liable to occur at this season, against the eating of oysters and clams, and also against the water of the canals. The euphemistic nature of the announcement was palpable. Groups of people had collected in silence on the bridge and squares; and the foreigner stood among them, scenting and brooding.

At a little shop he inquired about the repulsive smell,

asking the proprietor, who was leaning against his door surrounded by coral chains and imitation amethyst jewelry. The man measured him with heavy eyes, and brightened up hastily. "A matter of precaution, sir!" he answered with a gesture. "A regulation of the police which must be taken for what it is worth. This weather is oppressive, the sirocco is not good for the health. In short, you understand—an exaggerated prudence perhaps." Aschenbach thanked him and went on. Also on the steamer back to the Lido he caught the smell of the disinfectant.

Returning to the hotel, he went immediately to the periodical stand in the lobby and ran through the papers. He found nothing in the foreign-language press. The papers from home spoke of rumors, gave varying figures, repeated official denials and questioned their truthfulness. This explained the departure of the German and Austrian guests. Obviously, the subjects of the other nations knew nothing, suspected nothing, were not yet uneasy. "To keep it quiet!" Aschenbach thought excitedly, as he threw the papers back on the table. "To keep that quiet!" But at the same moment he was filled with satisfaction over the adventure that was to befall the world about him. For passion, like crime, does not agree with the secure daily rounds of order and well-being; and every slackening in the bourgeois structure, every disorder and affliction of the world, must be held welcome, since they bring with them a vague promise of advantage. So Aschenbach felt a dark contentment with what was taking place, under cover of the authorities, in the dirty alleys of Venice. This wicked secret of the city was welded with his own secret, and he too was involved in keeping it hidden. For in his infatuation he cared about nothing but the possibility of Tadzio's leaving, and he realized with something like terror that he would not know how to go on living if this occurred.

Lately he had not been relying simply on good luck and the daily routine for his chances to be near the boy and look at him. He pursued him, stalked him. On Sundays, for instance, the Poles never appeared on the beach. He guessed that they must be attending mass at San Marco. He hurried there; and, stepping from the heat of the square into the golden twilight of the church, he found the boy he was hunting, bowed over a prie-dieu, praying. Then he stood in the background, on the cracked mosaic floor, with people on all sides kneeling, murmuring, and making the sign of the cross. And the compact grandeur of this Oriental temple weighed heavily on his senses. In front, the richly ornamented priest was conducting the office, moving about and singing; incense poured forth, clouding the weak little flame of the candle on the altar—and with the sweet, stuffy sacrificial odor another seemed to commingle faintly: the smell of the infested city. But through the smoke and the sparkle Aschenbach saw how the boy there in front turned his head, looked for him, and found him.

When the crowd was streaming out through the opened portals into the brilliant square with its swarms of pigeons, the lover hid in the vestibule; he kept under cover, he lay in wait. He saw the Poles quit the church, saw how the children took ceremonious leave of their mother, and how she turned toward the Piazzetta on her way home. He made sure that the boy, the nunlike sisters, and the governess took the road to the right through the gateway of the clock tower and into the Merceria. And after giving them a slight start, he followed, followed them furtively on their walk through Venice. He had to stand still when they stopped; when they turned back, he hid in shops and courts to let them pass. He lost them; hot and exhausted, he hunted them over bridges and down dirty blind alleys— and he underwent minutes of deadly agony when suddenly he saw them coming toward him in a narrow passage where escape was impossible. Yet it could not be said that he suffered. He was drunk, and his steps followed the promptings of the demon who delights in treading human reason and dignity underfoot.

At one point Tadzio and his companions took a gondola; and shortly after they had pushed off from the shore, Aschenbach, who had hidden behind some structure, a well, while they were climbing in, would do the same. He spoke in a hurried undertone as he directed the rower, with the promise of a generous tip, to follow unnoticed and at a distance that gondola which was just rounding the corner. And he thrilled when the man, with the roguish willingness of a procurer, assured him in the same tone that his wishes would be carried out, carried out faithfully.

Leaning back against the soft black cushions, he rocked and glided toward the other black-beaked craft where his passion was drawing him. At times it escaped; then he felt worried and uneasy. But his pilot, as though skilled in such commissions, was always able through sly maneuvers, speedy diagonals and shortcuts, to bring the object of his quest into view again. The air was quiet and smelly, the sun burned down strong through the slate-colored mist. Water slapped against the wood and stone. The call of the gondolier, half warning, half greeting, was answered with a strange obedience far away in the silence of the labyrinth. White and purple umbels with the scent of almonds hung down from little elevated gardens over crumbling walls. Arabian window casings were outlined through the murkiness. The marble steps of a church descended into the water; a beggar squatted there, protesting his misery, holding out his hat, and showing the whites of his eyes as though he were blind. An antique-dealer in front of his den fawned on the passerby and invited him to stop in the hopes of swindling him. That was Venice, the flatteringly and suspiciously beautiful—this city, half legend, half snare for strangers; in its foul air art once flourished gluttonously, and had suggested to composers seductive notes which cradle and lull. The adventurer felt as though his eyes were taking in this same luxury, as though his ears were being wooed by just such melodies. He recalled too that the city was diseased and was concealing this through greed—and he peered more eagerly after the gondola that was gliding on before him.

Thus, in his infatuation, he wanted simply to pursue unceasingly the object that aroused him, to dream of it when it was not there, and, after the fashion of lovers, to speak softly to its mere shadow. Loneliness, strangeness, and the joy of a deep belated intoxication encouraged him and prompted him to accept even the oddest things without reserve or shame—and it so happened once that as he returned late in the evening from Venice, he stopped on the second floor of the hotel before the door of the boy's room, laid his head in utter drunkenness against the hinge of the door, and for a long time could not drag himself away despite the danger and confusion of being caught in such a mad situation.

Yet there were still moments when he paused and came partly to his senses. "Where to?" he would think, alarmed. "Where to?" Like every man whose natural abilities stimulate an aristocratic interest in his ancestry, he was accustomed to think of his forebears in connection with the accomplishments and successes of his life, to assure himself of their approval, their satisfaction, their necessary respect. He thought of them now, entangled as he was in such an illicit experience, caught in such exotic emotional excesses. He thought of their characteristic rigidity of principle, their scrupulous masculinity—and he smiled dejectedly. What would they say? But then, what would they have said to his whole life, which was almost degenerate in its departure from theirs, this life under the spell of art—a life against which he himself had once issued such youthful mockeries out of loyalty to his fathers, but which at bottom had been so much like theirs! He too had served, he too had been a soldier and a warrior like many of them—for art was a war, a destructive battle, and one was not equal to it for long, these days. A life of self-conquest and of in-spite-of's, a rigid, sober, and unyielding life which he had formed into the symbol of a delicate and timely heroism. He might well call it masculine, or brave; and it almost seemed as though the Eros that had got hold of him were somehow peculiarly appropriate to such a life. Had not this Eros stood in high repute among the bravest of peoples; was it not said that precisely through bravery he had flourished in their cities? Numerous war heroes of antiquity had willingly borne his yoke, for nothing was deemed a disgrace which the god imposed; and acts which would have been rebuked as the sign of cowardice if they had been done for other purposes—prostrations, oaths, entreaties, abjectness—such things did not bring shame upon the lover, but rather he reaped praise for them.

In this way his infatuation determined the course of his thoughts, in this way he tried to sustain himself, to keep his dignity. But at the same time he gave searching and persistent attention to the foul goings-on here in Venice, an adventure of the outer world which conspired darkly with his own, and which fed his passion with hopes vague and lawless.

Bent on getting reliable news of the condition and progress of the pestilence, he ransacked the papers from home in the city cafés, as they had been missing from the reading table of the hotel lobby for several days now. Statements alternated with disavowals. The number of the sick and dead was supposed to reach twenty, forty, or even a hundred and more—and immediately afterward every instance of the plague would be either flatly denied or attributed to completely isolated cases which had crept in from the outside. There were scattered admonitions, protests against the dangerous conduct of the local authorities. Certainty was impossible. Nevertheless, the lone man felt especially entitled to participate in the secret; and although he was excluded, he derived a grotesque satisfaction from putting embarrassing questions to those who did know, and, as they were pledged to silence, forcing them into deliberate lies. One day at breakfast in the large dining hall he entered into a conversation with the manager, that softly treading little man in the French frock coat who was moving amiably and solicitously about among the diners and had stopped at Aschenbach's table for a few passing words. Just why, the guest asked negligently and casually, had disinfectants become so prevalent in Venice recently? "It has to do," was the evasive answer, "with a police regulation, and is intended to prevent any inconveniences or disturbances to the public health which might result from the exceptionally warm and sultry weather." . . . "The police are to be congratulated," Aschenbach answered; and after the exchange of a few remarks on the weather, the manager left.

Yet that same day, in the evening, after dinner, it happened that a little band of strolling singers from the city gave a performance in the front garden of the hotel. Two men and two women, they stood by the iron post in the glare of an arc lamp and turned their brightly illumined faces up toward the large terrace where the guests were enjoying these popular songs over their coffee and cooling drinks. The hotel personnel, bellboys, waiters, and clerks from the office, could be seen listening by the doors of the vestibule. The Russian family, eager and precise in their amusements, had had wicker chairs placed in the garden in order to be nearer the performers; and they were sitting there in an appreciative semicircle. Behind the ladies and gentlemen, in her turbanlike kerchief, stood the old slave.

Mandolin, guitar, harmonica, and a squeaky violin were responding to the touch of the mendicant virtuosos. Instrumental numbers alternated with songs, as when the younger of the women, with a sharp trembling voice, joined with the sweetly falsetto tenor in a languishing love duet. But the real talent and leader of the group was undoubtedly the other of the two men, the one

with the guitar. He was a kind of *buffo* baritone, with
not much of a voice, although he did have a gift for
pantomime, and a remarkable comic energy. Often,
with his large instrument under his arm, he would leave
the rest of the group and, still acting, would intrude
on the platform, where his antics were rewarded with
encouraging laughter. The Russians in their seats down
front seemed to be especially enchanted with so much
southern mobility, and their applause incited him to
let himself out more and more boldly and assertively.

Aschenbach sat on the balustrade, cooling his lips
now and then with a mixture of pomegranate juice and
soda which glowed ruby-red in his glass in front of him.
His nerves took in the miserable notes, the vulgar croon-
ing melodies; for passion la ..es the sense of discrimina-
tion, and surrenders in all ·eriousness to appeals which,
in sober moments, are either humorously allowed for or
rejected with annoyanc.. At the clown's antics his features had twisted into a set painful smile. He sat there
as though relaxed, while inwardly beset with a most
exquisite attentiveness; for six paces in front of him,
leaning against the stone hand rail, stood Tadzio.

In the white belted coat which he often wore at mealtime, he was standing in a position of spontaneous and
inborn gracefulness, his left forearm on the railing, feet
crossed, the right hand resting on his hip; and he
looked down at the street singers with an expression
which was hardly a smile, but only an aloof curiosity,
a polite receptiveness. Often he would stand erect and,
expanding his chest, would draw the white smock down
under his leather belt with a beautiful gesture. And
then, too, the aging man observed with a tumult of
fright and triumph how he would often turn his head

over the left shoulder in the direction of his admirer,
carefully and hesitatingly, or even with abruptness as
though to attack by surprise. He did not meet Aschenbach's eyes, for a mean precaution compelled the trans-
gressor to keep from staring at him: in the background
of the terrace the women who guarded Tadzio were
sitting, and things had reached a point where the lover
had to fear he might be noticed and suspected. Yes, he
had often observed with a kind of numbness how, when
Tadzio was near him, on the beach, in the hotel lobby,
in the Piazza San Marco, they called him back, they
were set on keeping him at a distance—and this
wounded him frightfully, causing his pride unknown
tortures which his conscience would not permit him
to evade.

Meanwhile the guitar player had begun a solo to his
own accompaniment, a street ballad popular throughout
Italy. It had several strophes, and the entire company
joined each time in the refrain, all singing and playing,
while he managed to give a plastic and dramatic twist
to the performance. Of slight build, with thin and
haggard features, he stood on the gravel, apart from
his companions, in an attitude of insolent bravado, his
shabby felt hat on the back of his head so that a bunch
of his red hair jutted out from under the brim. And to
the thrumming of the strings he flung his jokes up at
the terrace in a penetrating recitative; while the veins
were swelling on his forehead from the exertion of his
performance. He did not seem of Venetian stock, but
rather of the race of Neapolitan comedians, half pimp,
half entertainer, brutal and audacious, dangerous and
amusing. His song was stupid enough so far as the words
went; but in his mouth, by his gestures, the movements

of his body, his way of blinking significantly and letting his tongue play lubriciously in the corner of his mouth, it acquired something ambiguous, something vaguely repulsive. In addition to the customary civilian dress, he was wearing a sport shirt; and his skinny neck protruded above the soft collar, baring a noticeably large and active Adam's apple. He was pale and snub-nosed. It was hard to fix an age to his beardless features, which seemed furrowed with grimaces and depravity; and the two wrinkles standing arrogantly, harshly, almost savagely between his reddish eyebrows were in strange contrast with the smirk on his mobile lips. Yet what really prompted the lonely man to pay him keen attention was the observation that the questionable figure seemed also to provide its own questionable atmosphere. For each time they came to the refrain the singer, amid buffoonery and familiar handshakes, began a grotesque circular march which brought him immediately beneath Aschenbach's place; and each time this happened, there blew up to the terrace from his clothes and body a strong carbolic smell.

After the song was ended, he began collecting money. He started with the Russians, who were evidently willing to spend, and then came up the stairs. Up here he showed himself just as humble as he had been bold during the performance. Cringing and bowing, he stole about among the tables, and a smile of obsequious cunning exposed his strong teeth, while the two wrinkles still stood ominously between his red eyebrows. This singular character collecting money to live on—they eyed him with a curiosity and a kind of repugnance, they tossed coins into his felt hat with the tips of their fingers, and were careful not to touch him. The elimination of the physical distance between the comedian and the audience, no matter how great the enjoyment may have been, always causes a certain uneasiness. He felt it, and tried to excuse it by groveling. He came up to Aschenbach, and along with him the smell, which no one else seemed concerned about.

"Listen!" the recluse said in an undertone, almost mechanically. "They are disinfecting Venice. Why?" The jester answered hoarsely: "On account of the police. That is a precaution, sir, with such heat, and the sirocco. The sirocco is oppressive. It is not good for the health." He spoke as though astonished that anyone could ask such things, and demonstrated with his open hand how oppressive the sirocco was. "Then there is no plague in Venice?" Aschenbach asked quietly, between his teeth. The clown's muscular features fell into a grimace of comical embarrassment. "A plague? What kind of plague? Perhaps our police are a plague? You like to joke! A plague! Of all things! A precautionary measure, you understand! A police regulation against the effects of the oppressive weather." He gesticulated. "Very well," Aschenbach replied curtly and quietly; and he quickly dropped an unduly large coin into the hat. Then with his eyes he signaled the man to leave. He obeyed, smirking and bowing. But he had not reached the stairs before two hotel employees threw themselves upon him, and with their faces close to his began a whispered cross-examination. He shrugged his shoulders; he gave assurances, he swore that he had kept quiet—that was evident. He was released, and he returned to the garden; then, after a short conference with his companions under the arc-lamp, he stepped out once more for a final song of thanks and leave-taking.

It was a rousing song which the recluse never recalled having heard before, a "big number" in incomprehensible dialect, with a laugh refrain in which the troupe joined regularly at the top of their voices. At this point both the words and the accompaniment of the instruments stopped, with nothing left but a laugh which was somehow arranged rhythmically although very naturally done—and the soloist especially showed great talent in giving it a most deceptive vitality. At the renewal of his professional distance from the audience, he recovered all his boldness again, and the artificial laugh that he directed up toward the terrace was derisive. Even before the end of the articulate portion of the strophe, he seemed to struggle against an irresistible tickling. He gulped, his voice trembled, he pressed his hand over his mouth, he contorted his shoulders; and at the proper moment the ungovernable laugh broke out of him, burst into such real cackles that it was infectious and communicated itself to the audience, so that on the terrace also an unfounded hilarity, living off itself alone, started up. But this seemed to double the singer's exuberance. He bent his knees, he slapped his thighs, he nearly split himself; he no longer laughed, he shrieked. He pointed up with his finger, as though nothing were more comic than the laughing guests there, and finally everyone in the garden and on the veranda was laughing, even including the waiters, bellboys, and house servants in the doorways.

Aschenbach was no longer resting in his chair; he sat upright, as if attempting to defend himself, or to escape

But the laughter, the whiffs of the hospital smell, and the boy's nearness combined to put him into a trance that held his mind and his senses hopelessly captive. In the general movement and distraction he ventured to glance across at Tadzio, and as he did so he dared observe that the boy, in reply to his glance, was equally serious, much as though he had modeled his conduct and expression after those of one man, and the prevalent mood had no effect on him since this one man was not part of it. This portentous childish obedience had something so disarming and overpowering about it that the gray-haired man could hardly restrain himself from burying his face in his hands. It had also seemed to him that Tadzio's occasional stretching and quick breathing indicated a complaint, a congestion, of the lungs. "He is sickly, he will probably not grow old," he thought repeatedly with that positiveness which is often a peculiar relief to desire and passion. And along with pure solicitude he had a feeling of rakish gratification.

Meanwhile the Venetians had ended and were leaving. Applause accompanied them, and their leader did not miss the opportunity to cover his retreat with further jests. His bows, the kisses he blew, were laughed at—and so he doubled them. When his companions were already gone, he acted as though he had hurt himself by backing into a lamppost, and he crept through the gate seemingly crippled with pain. Then he suddenly threw off the mask of comic hard luck, stood upright, hurried away jauntily, stuck out his tongue insolently at the guests on the terrace, and slipped into the darkness. The company was breaking up; Tadzio had been missing from the balustrade for some time. But, to the displeasure of the waiters, the lonely man sat for a long while over the remains of his pomegranate drink. Night advanced. Time was crumbling. In the house of his parents many years back, there had been an hourglass— of a sudden he saw the fragile and expressive instrument again, as though it were standing in front of him. Fine and noiseless, the rust-red sand was running through the glass neck; and since it was getting low in the upper half, an urgent little vortex had been formed there.

As early as the following day, in the afternoon, he had made new progress in his obstinate baiting of the people he met—and this time he had all possible success. He walked from the Piazza San Marco into the English travel bureau located there; and after changing some money at the cash desk, he put on the expression of a distrustful foreigner and launched his fatal question at the attendant clerk. He was a Britisher; he wore a woolen suit, and was still young, with his hair parted in the middle, and with close-set eyes, and had that characteristic stolid reliability which is so peculiarly and strikingly appealing in the tricky, nimble-witted South. He began: "No reason for alarm, sir. A regulation without any serious significance. Such measures are often taken to anticipate the unhealthy effects of the heat and the sirocco. . . ." But as he raised his blue eyes, he met the stare of the foreigner, a tired and somewhat unhappy stare focused on his lips with a touch of scorn. Then the Englishman blushed. "At least," he continued in an emotional undertone, "that is the official explanation which people see fit to go along with. I can tell you that there is something more behind it." And then in his forthright, easy-going English, he told the truth.

For several years now Asiatic cholera had shown a heightened tendency to spread and migrate. Hatched in the warm swamps of the Ganges delta, rising with the noxious breath of that luxuriant, uninhabitable primitive world and island wilderness which is shunned by humans and where the tiger crouches in the bamboo thickets, the plague had raged continuously and with unusual strength in Hindustan, had reached eastward to China, westward to Afghanistan and Persia, and, following the chief caravan routes, had carried its terrors to Astrakhan, and even to Moscow. But while Europe was trembling lest the specter continue its advance from there by land, it had been transported over the sea in Syrian merchantmen, and had turned up almost simultaneously in several Mediterranean ports, had raised its head in Toulon and Málaga, had showed its mask several times in Palermo and Naples, and seemed permanently entrenched through Calabria and Apulia. The north of the peninsula had been spared. Yet in the middle of this May in Venice the frightful vibrions were found on one and the same day in the blackish wasted bodies of a cabin boy and a woman who sold green-groceries. The cases were kept secret. But within a week there were ten, twenty, thirty more, and in various sections. A man from the Austrian provinces who had made a pleasure trip to Venice for a few days returned to his home town and died with unmistakable symptoms—and that is how the first reports of the pestilence in the lagoon city got into the German newspapers. The Venetian authorities answered that the city's health conditions had never been better, and took the most necessary preventive measures. But probably the food supply—vegetables, meat, or milk—had been

infected. Denied and glossed over, death was eating its
way along the narrow streets, and its dissemination was
especially favored by the premature summer heat which
warmed the water of the canal. Yes, it seemed as
though the plague had got renewed strength, as though
the tenacity and fertility of its powers had doubled.
Cases of recovery were rare. Out of a hundred attacks,
eighty were fatal, and in the most horrible manner. For
the plague moved with utter savagery, and often showed
that most dangerous form which is called "the drying."
Water from the blood vessels collected in pockets, and
the blood was unable to carry this off. Within a few
hours the victim was parched, his blood became as thick
as glue, and he stifled amid cramps and hoarse groans.
Lucky for him if, as sometimes happened, the attack
took the form of a light discomfiture followed by a profound coma from which he seldom or never awakened.
At the beginning of June the quarantine wards of the
Ospedale Civico had quietly filled; there was not much
room left in the two orphan asylums, and a frightfully
active commerce was kept up between the wharf of the
Fondamente Nuove and San Michele, the burial island.
But there was the fear of a general drop in prosperity.
The recently opened art exhibit in the public gardens
was to be considered, along with the heavy losses which,
in case of panic or damaging rumors, would threaten
business, the hotels, the entire elaborate tourist trade
—and as these considerations evidently carried more
weight than love of truth or respect for international
agreements, the city authorities upheld obstinately
their policy of silence, and denial. The chief health
officer had resigned from his post in indignation, and
had been promptly replaced by a more tractable per-

sonality. The people knew this; and the corruption of their superiors, together with the prevailing insecurity, the exceptional condition into which the city had been plunged by death, led to a certain demoralization of the lower classes, encouraging shady and antisocial impulses which manifested themselves in license, profligacy, and a rising crime wave. Contrary to custom, many drunkards were seen in the evenings; it was said that at night nasty mobs made the streets unsafe. Burglaries and even murders became frequent, for it had already been proved on two occasions that persons who had presumably fallen victim to the plague had in reality been dispatched with poison by their own relatives. And professional debauchery assumed abnormal obtrusive proportions such as had never been known here before, and to an extent which is usually found only in the southern parts of the country and in the Orient.

On these matters the Englishman mentioned the decisive points. Then, "You would do well," he concluded, "to leave today rather than tomorrow. It cannot be much more than a couple of days before a quarantine is declared."

"Thank you," Aschenbach said, and left the office.

The square lay sunless and stifling. Unsuspecting foreigners sat in front of the cafés or stood, covered with pigeons, in front of the church and watched the swarms of birds flapping their wings, crowding one another, and pecking at grains of corn offered them in open palms. The recluse was feverishly excited, triumphant in his possession of the truth. But it had left him with a bad taste in his mouth, and a weird horror in his heart. As he walked up and down the flagstones of the magnificent court, he was weighing an action which would meet the situation and would absolve him. This evening after dinner he could approach the woman with the pearls and make her a speech; he had figured it out word for word: "Permit a foreigner, madam, to give you some useful advice, a warning, which is being withheld from you through self-interest. Leave immediately with Tadzio and your daughters! Venice is plague-ridden." Then he could lay a farewell hand on the head of this tool of a mocking divinity, turn away, and flee this morass. But he felt at the same time that he was very far from seriously desiring such a move. It would lead him back, would restore him to himself; but to one who is beside oneself, nothing is more abhorrent than any such restoration. He recalled a white building, ornamented with inscriptions which glistened in the evening and in whose transparent mysticism his mind's eye had lost itself—and then that strange wanderer's form which had awakened in the aging man the roving hankerings of youth after the foreign and the remote. And thoughts of returning home, of prudence, soberness, effort, mastery, disgusted him to such an extent that his face was distorted with an expression of physical nausea. "It must be kept quiet!" he whispered fiercely. And: "I will keep quiet!" The awareness of his complicity, his partnership in this guilty knowledge, intoxicated him, much as a little wine intoxicates a tired brain. The picture of the diseased and neglected city hovering desolately before him aroused vague hopes beyond the bounds of reason, but with an egregious sweetness. What was the scant happiness he had dreamed of a moment ago compared with these expectations? What were art and virtue worth to him over against the advantages of chaos? He kept quiet, and remained in Venice.

This same night he had a frightful dream, if one can designate as a dream a bodily and mental experience which occurred to him in the deepest sleep, completely independent of him, and with a physical realness, although he never saw himself present or moving about among the incidents; but their stage rather was his soul itself, and they broke in from without, trampling down his resistance—a profound and spiritual resistance—by sheer force; and when they had passed through, they left his substance, the culture of his lifetime, crushed and annihilated behind them.

It began with anguish, anguish and desire, and a frightened curiosity as to what was coming. It was night, and his senses were on the watch. From far off a grumble, an uproar, was approaching, a jumble of noises. Clanking, blaring, and dull thunder, with shrill shouts and a definite whine in a long-drawn-out *u*-sound—all this was sweetly, ominously interspersed with and dominated by the deep cooing of wickedly persistent flutes which charmed the bowels in a shamelessly intrusive manner. But he knew one phrase; it was veiled, and yet would name what was approaching: "The strange god!" Vaporous fire began to glow; then he recognized mountains like those about his summer house. And in the scattered light, from high up in the woods, among tree trunks and crumbling moss-grown rocks—people, beasts, a throng, a raging mob plunged twisting and whirling downward, and made the slope swarm with bodies, flames, tumult, and a riotous round dance. Women, tripped by overlong fur draperies which hung from their waists, were holding up tambourines

and beating on them, their groaning heads flung back.
Others swung sparking firebrands and bare daggers, or
wore hissing snakes about the middle of their bodies,
or, shrieking, held their breasts in their two hands.
Men with horns on their foreheads, shaggy-haired,
girded with hides, bent back their necks and raised
their arms and thighs, clashed brass cymbals and beat
furiously at kettledrums, while smooth boys prodded
he-goats with wreathed sticks, climbing on their horns
and falling off with shouts when they bounded. And the
bacchantes wailed the word with the soft consonants
and the drawn-out *u*-sound, at once sweet and savage,
like nothing ever heard before. Here it rang out as
though piped into the air by stags, and it was echoed
there by many voices, in wild triumph—with it they
incited one another to dance and to fling out their
arms and legs, and it was never silent. But everything
was pierced and dominated by the deep coaxing flute.
He who was fighting against this experience—did it not
coax him too, with its shameless persistence, into the
feast and the excesses of the extreme sacrifice? His repugnance, his fear, were keen—he was honorably set
on defending himself to the very last against the bar-
barian, the foe to intellectual poise and dignity. But
the noise, the howling, multiplied by the resonant walls
of the hills, grew, took the upper hand, swelled to a
fury of rapture. Odors oppressed the senses, the pungent
smell of the bucks, the scent of moist bodies, and a waft
of stagnant water, with another smell, something familiar, the smell of wounds and disease. At the beating
of the drum his heart fluttered, his head was spinning,
he was caught in a frenzy, in a blinding deafening lewd-
ness—and he yearned to join the ranks of the god. The

obscene symbol, huge, wooden, was uncovered and raised up; then they howled the magic word with more abandon. Foaming at the mouth, they raged, teased one another with ruttish gestures and caressing hands; laughing and groaning, they stuck the goads into one another's flesh and licked the blood from their limbs. But the dreamer now was with them, in them, and he belonged to the strange god. Yes, he and they were one, as they hurled themselves biting and tearing upon the animals, devoured steaming bits of flesh, and fell in promiscuous union on the torn moss, in sacrifice to their god. And his soul tasted the unchastity and fury of decay.

When he awakened from the affliction of this dream, he was unnerved, shattered, and hopelessly under the power of the demon. He no longer avoided the inquisitive glances of other people; he did not care if he was exciting their suspicions. And as a matter of fact, they were fleeing, traveling elsewhere. Numerous cabins stood empty, there were more and more empty tables in the dining hall, and in the city now one rarely saw a foreigner. The truth seemed to have leaked out; close-mouthed as those had been whose interests were involved, the panic seemed no longer avoidable. But the woman with the pearls remained with her family, either because the rumors had not yet reached her or because she was too proud and fearless to heed them. Tadzio remained. And to Aschenbach, in his infatuation, it seemed at times as though flight and death might remove all the disturbing elements of life around them and leave him here alone with the boy. Yes, by the sea in the forenoon when his eyes rested heavily, irresponsibly, unwaveringly on the object of his desire, or when, as the day was ending, he followed shamelessly after him through streets where the hideous death lurked in secret—at such times the atrocious seemed to him rich in promises, and the moral law seemed in ruins.

Like any lover, he wanted to please; and he felt a bitter anguish lest it might not be possible. He added bright youthful details to his dress, he put on jewels, and used perfumes. During the day he often spent much time over his toilet, and came to the table strikingly dressed, excited, and in suspense. In the light of the sweet youthfulness which had done this to him, he detested his aging body. The sight of his gray hair, his sharp features, plunged him into shame and hopelessness. It induced him to attempt rejuvenating his body and appearance. He often visited the hotel barber.

Beneath the barber's apron, leaning back in the chair under the gossiper's expert hands, he winced to observe his reflection in the mirror.

"Gray," he said, making a wry face.

"A little," the man answered. "Due entirely to a slight neglect, an indifference to outward things, which is conceivable in people of importance, but it is not exactly praiseworthy. And all the less so since such persons are above prejudice in matters of nature or art. If the moral objections of certain people to the art of cosmetics were to be logically extended to the care of the teeth, they would give no slight offense. And after all, we are just as old as we feel, and under some circumstances gray hair would actually stand for more of an untruth than the despised correction. In your case, sir, you are entitled to the natural color of your hair. Will you permit me simply to return what belongs to you?"

"How is that?" Aschenbach asked.

Then, to cap his eloquence, the man washed his client's hair with two kinds of water, one clear and one dark, and it was as black as in youth. Following this, he curled it with irons into soft waves, stepped back, and eyed his work.

"All that is left now," he said, "would be to freshen up the skin a little."

And like someone who cannot finish, cannot satisfy himself, he passed with quickening energy from one manipulation to another. Aschenbach rested comfortably, incapable of resistance, or rather his hopes were aroused by what was taking place. In the glass he saw his brows arch more evenly and decisively. His eyes became longer; their brilliance was heightened by a light touching up of the lids. A little lower, where the skin had been a leatherish brown, he saw a delicate crimson tint grow beneath a deft application of color. His lips, bloodless a little while past, became full, and as red as raspberries. The furrows in the cheeks and about the mouth, the wrinkles of the eyes, disappeared beneath lotions and cream. With a knocking heart he beheld a blossoming youth. Finally the beauty specialist declared himself content, after the manner of such people, by obsequiously thanking the man he had been serving. "A trifling aid," he said, as he applied one parting touch. "Now the gentleman can fall in love unhesitatingly." He walked away, fascinated; he was happy as in a dream, timid and bewildered. His necktie was red, his broad-brimmed straw hat was trimmed with a variegated band.

A tepid storm wind had risen. It was raining sparsely and at intervals, but the air was damp, thick, and filled with the smell of things rotting. All around him he

heard a fluttering, pattering, and swishing; and in a
fever under his cosmetics, he felt as though wind-
demons were haunting the place, impure sea birds
which rooted and gnawed at the food of the con-
demned and befouled it with their droppings. For the
sultriness destroyed his appetite, and the fancy suggested itself that the foods were poisoned with con-
taminating substances. Tracking the boy one afternoon,
Aschenbach had plunged deep into the tangled center
of the diseased city. He was becoming uncertain of
where he was, since the alleys, waterways, bridges, and
little squares of the labyrinth were all so much alike,
and he was no longer even sure of directions. He was
absorbed with the problem of keeping the pursued figure
in sight. And, driven to disgraceful subterfuges, flatten-
ing himself against walls, hiding behind the backs of
other people, for a long time he did not notice the
weariness, the exhaustion, with which emotion and the
continual suspense had taxed his mind and his body.
Tadzio walked behind the rest of his group. He always
allowed the governess and the nunlike sisters to precede
him in the narrow places; and, sauntering alone,
he would turn his head occasionally to look over his
shoulder and make sure by a glance of his peculiarly
dark-gray eyes that his admirer was following. He saw
him, and did not betray him. Drunk with the knowledge
of this, lured forward by those eyes, led meekly by his
passion, the lover stole after his unseemly hope—but
finally he was cheated and lost sight of him. The Poles
had crossed a short arching bridge; the height of the
curve hid them from the pursuer, and when he himself
had arrived there he no longer saw them. He hunted
for them vainly in three directions, straight ahead and

to either side along the narrow dirty wharf. In the end he was so tired and unnerved that he had to give up the search.

His head was on fire, his body was covered with a sticky sweat, he trembled. He could no longer endure the thirst that was torturing him, and he looked around for some immediate relief. From a little vegetable store he bought some fruit—strawberries, soft and overly ripe—and he ate them as he walked. A charmed, forsaken little square opened up before him. He recognized it; here he had made his frustrated plans for flight weeks ago. He let himself sink down on the steps of the cistern in the middle of the square, and laid his head against the stone cylinder. It was quiet; grass was growing up through the pavement; refuse was scattered about. Among the weather-beaten, irregularly tall houses surrounding him there was one like a palace, with little lion-covered balconies and Gothic windows with blank emptiness behind them. On the ground floor of another house was a pharmacy. Warm gusts of wind occasionally carried the smell of carbolic acid.

He sat there, he, the master, the artist of dignity, the author of *The Wretch*, a work which had, in such accurate symbols, renounced vagabondage and the murky depths of misery, had denied all sympathy with the abyss, and had cast out the outcast; the man who had arrived and, victor over his own knowledge, had outgrown all irony and acclimatized himself to the obligations of public confidence; whose reputation was official, whose name had been knighted, and on whose style boys were urged to pattern themselves—he sat there. His eyelids were shut; only now and then a mocking uneasy side glance slipped out from beneath them. And his loóse lips, set off by the cosmetics, formed isolated words of the strange dream logic created by his half-slumbering brain.

"For beauty, Phaedrus, mark me, beauty alone is both divine and visible at once; and thus it is the road of the sensuous; it is, little Phaedrus, the road of the artist to the spiritual. But do you now believe, my dear, that they can ever attain wisdom and true human dignity for whom the road to the spiritual leads through the senses? Or do you believe rather (I leave the choice to you) that this is a pleasant but perilous road, a really wrong and sinful road, which necessarily leads astray? For you must know that we poets cannot take the road of beauty without having Eros join us and set himself up as our leader. Indeed, we may even be heroes after our fashion, and hardened warriors; and yet we are like women, for passion is our exaltation, and our desire must remain love—that is our pleasure and our disgrace. You now see, do you not, that we poets cannot be wise and dignified? That we necessarily go astray, necessarily remain lascivious, and adventurers in emotion? The mastery of our style is all lies and foolishness, our renown and honor are a farce, the confidence of the masses in us is highly ridiculous, and the training of the public and of youth through art is a precarious undertaking which should be forbidden. For how, indeed, could he be a fit instructor who is born with a natural leaning toward the abyss? We might well disavow it and reach after dignity, but wherever we turn it attracts us. Let us, say, renounce the dissolvent of knowledge, since knowledge, Phaedrus, has no dignity or strength. It is aware, it understands and pardons, without reservation and form. It feels sympathy with the abyss, it *is* the abyss. This, then, we abandon with firmness, and from now on our efforts arc directed solely toward beauty, or, in other words, simplicity, greatness, and new rigor, form, and a reborn innocence. But form and innocence, Phaedrus, lead to intoxication and to desire, lead the noble perhaps into sinister revels of emotion which his own beautiful rigor rejects as infamous, lead to the abyss—yes, they too lead to the abyss. They lead us poets thus, I say, since we cannot lift ourselves up, and can but let ourselves loose. And now I am going, Phaedrus. You stay here; and when you no longer see me, then you go too."

A few days later, as Gustav von Aschenbach was not feeling well, he left the Beach Hotel at a later hour in the morning than usual. He had to fight against certain attacks of vertigo which were only partially physical and were accompanied by a sharply mounting dread, a feeling of bafflement and hopelessness—while he was not certain whether this had to do with conditions outside him or within. In the lobby he noticed a large pile of luggage ready for shipment; he asked the doorkeeper who it was that was leaving, and heard in answer the Polish title which he had learned secretly. He accepted this without any alteration of his sunken features, with that curt elevation of the head by which one acknowledges something one does not need to know. Then he asked: "When?" The answer was: "After lunch." He nodded, and went to the beach.

It was not very inviting. Rippling patches of rain retreated across the wide flat water separating the beach from the first long sandbank. An air of autumn, of things past their prime, seemed to lie over the pleasure spot which had once been so alive with color and was now almost abandoned. The sand was no longer kept clean. A camera, seemingly without an owner, stood on its tripod by the edge of the sea; and a black cloth thrown over it was flapping noisily in the wind.

Tadzio, with the three or four companions still left, was moving about to the right in front of his family's cabin. And midway between the sea and the row of cabins, lying back in his chair with a robe over his knees, Aschenbach looked at him once more. The game, which was not being supervised since the women were probably occupied with preparations for the journey, seemed to have no rules, and it was degenerating. The stocky boy with the sleek black hair who was called Jaschu had been angered and blinded by sand flung in his face. He forced Tadzio into a wrestling match which quickly ended in the fall of the beauty, who was weaker. But as though, in the hour of parting, the servile feelings of the inferior had turned to merciless brutality and were trying to get vengeance for a long period of slavery, the victor did not let go of the boy underneath, but knelt on his back and pressed his face so persistently into the sand that Tadzio, already breathless from the struggle, was in danger of strangling. His attempts to shake off the weight were fitful; for moments they stopped entirely and were resumed again as mere twitchings. Terrified. Aschenbach was about to spring to the rescue, when the torturer finally released his victim. Tadzio, very pale, raised himself halfway and sat motionless for several minutes, resting on one arm, with rumpled hair and glowering eyes. Then he stood up completely, and moved slowly away. They called him, cheerfully at first, then anxiously and imploringly; he did not listen. The swarthy boy, who seemed to regret his excesses immediately afterward, caught up with him and tried to placate him. A movement of the shoulder put him at his distance. Tadzio went down obliquely to the water. He was barefoot, and wore his striped linen suit with the red bow.

He lingered on the edge of the water with his head down, tracing figures in the wet sand with one toe; then he went into the shallows which, even at their deepest, did not come up to his knees; and after a leisurely crossing he arrived at the sandbank. He stood there a moment, his face turned to the open sea; soon after, he began stepping slowly to the left along the narrow stretch of exposed ground. Separated from the mainland by the expanse of water, separated from his companions by a proud moodiness, he walked on, a starkly isolated and remote figure with fluttering hair—placed out there in the sea, and the wind, against a boundless haze. He stopped once more to look around. And suddenly, as though at some recollection, some impulse, with one hand on his hip and without shifting his basic posture, he made a lovely twist with the upper part of his body, and glanced over his shoulder toward the shore. The watcher sat there, as he had sat once before when for the first time these twilight-gray eyes had turned at that threshold and met his own. His head, against the back of the chair, had slowly followed the movements of the boy walking yonder. Now, as if to meet that glance, it rose and then sank on his breast, so that his eyes looked out from beneath, while his face took on the relaxed, inward-turning expression of deep sleep. The pale and lovely Summoner out there seemed as though smiling to him, beckoning, as if, removing his hand from his hip, he were calling him to cross over, vaguely guiding him toward some prodigious fulfillment. And, as so often before, he rose to follow.

Some minutes passed before anyone hurried to the aid of the man who, as he sat there, had collapsed into one corner of his chair. He was brought to his room. And on the same day a respectfully shocked world received the news of his death.

AUTOBIOGRAPHY
AND LITERATURE*

BY *Erich Heller*

1

THE autobiographical elements in *Death in Venice* are
so obvious that they would hardly be worth discussing
for their own sake; yet to attend to them means at the
same time to contemplate something that is of greater
interest than they are in themselves, namely, Thomas
Mann's art of writing and thus some aspects of the art

---

* Most of the quotations—except, of course, those from *Death in
Venice*—come from works or letters of Thomas Mann that have
not been translated into English. In these cases the translations
are my own. The numbers in parentheses that follow quotations
refer to volumes and pages of the German edition of Thomas
Mann's *Collected Works*, 12 volumes, Frankfurt a.M., 1960.
Thomas Mann's letters are quoted from the edition made by
Erika Mann, 3 volumes, Frankfurt a.M., 1961, 1963, and 1965.
For quotations from notebooks in the Thomas Mann Archive
I am indebted to Herbert Lehnert's book, *Thomas Mann: Fiction,
Mythos, Religion*, Stuttgart, 1965, and to Hans Wysling's article,
"Aschenbachs Werke" in the 59th volume of *Euphorion, a Journal
for the History of Literature*, Heidelberg, 1965, pp. 272 ff. Also, I
have not been able to avoid a few borrowings from my own book
Thomas Mann: The Ironic German.

of writing as such. It is pleasurable as well as illuminating to watch Thomas Mann as he transforms "life," his life, into what Nietzsche called an "aesthetic phenomenon," a sensible composition in which every fragment falls into its seemingly preordained place, thus redeeming what as merely "lived" experience may appear to be accidental and fragmentary. This he does by what sometimes looks like (but never is) a mere record of the experience itself, entrusting its artistic metamorphosis to the recorder's tone of voice, its rhythms, inflections and cadences: in brief, his style. Then again he merges what has happened in his own life with occurrences in other lives, related to his by real similarity or else chosen by him as "mythological" models, lives upon which myth or history has already bestowed representative or symbolic stature. However, this "mythologizing" soon begins to modify the "live" experience of the artist by coloring it with the tints of art, so that in the end we are no longer quite sure how much had to be "transformed." Indeed, a writer like Thomas Mann (or Proust or Joyce) comes to experience a great deal of what for other people would simply be "life" as, from the outset, *aesthetic* experience, as representative, mythological, or symbolic, in short, as "literature." Franz Kafka once rejected with indignant irony a graphologist's assertion, on examining his handwriting, that he had "literary interests." "No," Kafka exclaimed, "I have no literary interests; I *am* literature!" This might profitably be remembered whenever the discussion of Thomas Mann's works—and of much else in modern literature—reaches the inevitable point at which life and art come into view as eternally inimical opposites.

Death in Venice tells the story of Gustav von Aschenbach, a writer, and thus the autobiographical element becomes all but unavoidable. And it would certainly be surprising—after the blatantly autobiographical *Tonio Kröger*, Thomas Mann's "Portrait of the Artist as a Young Man"—if the points of identity between author and hero were limited to their vocation, or, for that matter, to the initial "L" of their birthplaces. The second chapter of *Death in Venice* is entirely devoted to Aschenbach's biography, to his life as a writer: for he has had no other life—a fact which is the necessary condition for the tale told. Right at the beginning of this biographical second chapter, it becomes clear that Thomas Mann allowed his fictional author to become famous through works that he himself had intended to produce at one time or another and instead vicariously completed through Aschenbach. From Thomas Mann's notebooks (assembled in the Thomas Mann Archive in Zürich), we now know that he had himself planned to write "Maya," one of Aschenbach's masterpieces, as well as the "stark tale . . . called 'The Wretch,'" a story which taught a new generation that moral certainty was still attainable despite our new awareness of relative, conditional, and "psychological" truths. Ironically enough, this "certainty" is tragically brought into question by the story of *Death in Venice*.

Of Aschenbach's impassioned and yet learned treatise on "Art and the Spirit," that great essay which even "cautious" judges would "place alongside" Schiller's celebrated reflections "On Naive and Sentimental Poetry," we have at least a fragment written by Thomas Mann at about the time of *Death in Venice* and published under the title of "The Artist and the

Man of Letters" (X, 62 ff.). And from the "lucid and powerful prose epic" that Aschenbach "built around the life of Frederick of Prussia," Thomas Mann, after abandoning the project of the Frederick novel, took for himself as much as he could accommodate within the limits of his brilliant and controversial essay on "Frederick and the Great Coalition."

But in fact, we learn nothing of Aschenbach's writings that does not confirm the literary identity of Gustav von Aschenbach and Thomas Mann. The heroes of Aschenbach's fictional world are Thomas Mann's own heroes: those "moralists of accomplishment" who, always a little like his Frederick of Prussia, are "modern" heroes by virtue of their almost abstractly moral wills driving them on to achievements the "meaning" of which they regard with the same skepticism as "the meaning of life" itself. When, for instance, Thomas Mann says that one of Aschenbach's characters, with elegance and supreme self-control, succeeded in concealing from the eyes of the world how precariously undermined his existence had become through both inner uncertainties and biological decay, he clearly has in mind his own Thomas Buddenbrook. Or he undoubtedly thinks of his two central figures in *Fiorenza*, Lorenzo de'Medici and Savonarola, when he describes two of Aschenbach's imaginary creations: one as a man who, although nature had made him into an ugly sensualist, yet triumphed by pacifying his passions and setting up his kingdom of sheer beauty; the other as a pale and weak creature who, from the depth of his mind, drew the strength to conquer with the Cross a whole people, exuberant and proud. And surely it is to the young prince, hero of the comedy-novel *Royal*

Highness, that Thomas Mann alludes when he names
as one of Aschenbach's themes that graceful bearing
which a man must preserve even in the rigid exercise
of duties he feels to be vacuous and outdated; or to
Felix Krull, when he makes Aschenbach write about
the false and perilous life and the firework artistry of
a born impostor.

The urge surreptitiously to lift the pseudonym and
confess his identity with some of his heroes sometimes
assumes the form of a mystifying playfulness which
Thomas Mann indulged so generously that it is likely
to stir into action ever bigger swarms of literary detec-
tives for years to come. In that biographical second
chapter of *Death in Venice*, he speaks for instance of
Aschenbach's belief, treated again and again in his own
fiction, that "nearly everything great which comes into
being does so in spite of something—in spite of sorrow
or suffering, poverty, destitution, physical weakness,
depravity, passion, or a thousand other handicaps,"
a conviction which it is said Aschenbach expressed once
directly in an inconspicuous place. Why, the reader
may well ask, the pedantic mention of the "inconspicuous place"? Because he, Thomas Mann himself, had
used these very words, six years before he gave them to
Aschenbach, in answering a question that a rather
"inconspicuous" journal had put to a number of artist
about alcohol as a creative stimulant (XI, 718).

Yet while such asides proclaim, or perhaps whisper,
"It is I," the revelation may be withdrawn again as if
it had been made at a moment of excessive intimacy,
or else to ward off the misunderstanding that the "I"
of a work of art could truly be the same as the "I" of
the real person. No, "art is a heightened mode of exist-

ence." Thomas Mann says this right at the end of the
chapter that so intriguingly blends fictional biography
with real autobiography; and so, with a determined
literary gesture, he breaks off the autobiographical line
he had just drawn. It is as if he wished to say: Of course,
this story may never have been told had its author, in
his real life, not had certain experiences; but it would
be folly to assume that in his writing he simply reports
them. The "I" of literature does not belong to the
domain of "reality"; it is a citizen of the realm of art.
Therefore, having unmistakably pointed to the same-
ness of the real and the fictional author, of Thomas
Mann and Gustav von Aschenbach, he now describes
the face of Aschenbach after the image of an artist very
different from himself in appearance and work; and he
does so with such realistic suggestiveness that a litho-
graph, made about ten years later by an illustrator of
Death in Venice, shows Aschenbach's head as strikingly
resembling—Gustav Mahler.

"When I first saw it, I was almost terrified," wrote
Thomas Mann in 1921. Why Gustav Mahler? The
answer, paradoxically, gives yet another touch of autobiography to what may have been designed to stress
the universal meaning of the story by distracting from
its autobiographical nature. For at about the time he
conceived the story, in the spring of 1911, Thomas
Mann heard of the composer's death; only shortly
before, he had made Mahler's acquaintance in Munich
and was deeply impressed by his "self-consuming in-
tensity." Now the shock of the sad news "mingled with
the impressions and ideas that brought forth the story."
This was the reason why he gave to his hero, who would
die in a state of ecstatic abandon, not only the first
name of the composer, but his features as well, feeling

sure that his readers, unaware of the creative coincidence, would never recognize the likeness (XI, 582 ff.).

The story was written between the summers of 1911 and 1912, and was first published by *Die Neue Rundschau* in the autumn of 1912. We shall never know for certain what the impressions were that "brought forth" the story. Yet again it is fascinating and instructive to observe the autobiographical hide-and-seek that Thomas Mann is so fond of playing in the unreliable border-region between the empirical and the imaginative truth.

Thomas Mann's Tonio Kröger, we remember, bitterly complained that emotional aloofness, indeed, coldness on the part of the writer was a necessary condition of his successfully rendering in literature the life of the passions. This was in fact the theme of *Tonio Kröger*. To dedicate oneself to writing is to freeze one's own feelings; it follows therefore that the poem that formed itself in Tonio's mind during a nocturnal sea voyage when "his heart was alive" was bad and useless; and it was bad and useless *because* he "felt." *Death in Venice*, in turn, is the story of an artist's frozen feelings destructively released by a sudden thaw that makes them flood the soul and annihilate the person.

A little scene in the third chapter of *Death in Venice* supports the Tonio "dogma." Aschenbach, having just arrived in his Lido hotel after a somewhat ominous crossing from another Adriatic resort, set eyes for the first time on the Polish boy Tadzio, and saw with surprise that he possessed that perfect beauty which recalls "Greek sculpture of the noblest period." During the lengthy dinner that evening, sitting alone and at some distance from the Polish family, Aschenbach now entertains himself with speculations about beauty, form, and art, only to discover at the end that "his thoughts . . . were like the seemingly felicitous promptings of a dream which, when the mind is sobered, are seen to be completely empty." Like Tonio Kröger on that ship, his emotions, stirred by Tadzio's beauty, are now alive, and his literary thoughts are therefore without value. Thomas Mann may even have been suggesting the measure of Aschenbach's emotional state by mentioning the feebleness, at that point, of his aesthetic findings.

Yet as if afterwards to disprove the Tonio Kröger "doctrine," Thomas Mann shows in the fourth chapter how Aschenbach, at the height of his passion for Tadzio, is suddenly seized by a desire to write, and how he does so on the beach and in the sight of Tadzio, deriving from the boy's beauty both his inspiration and his criterion of artistic perfection. Emotional detachment no longer seems to count as the sole condition of good writing; on the contrary, it is, we are told, a short piece of exquisite prose that Aschenbach produces by thus communing with his beloved. After all, Goethe wrote one of his greatest poems, the Marienbad "Elegy," immediately upon his parting with Ulrike von Levetzow, and called it (to Eckermann, 16 November 1823) "the product of a highly impassioned condition." The greatest happiness of a writer lies now, or so we read in *Death in Venice*, in thoughts that may wholly be transformed into feelings, in feelings that may wholly enter into thoughts. Passion and intellectual articulation are at one.*

---

* It is a strange accident of literary history that T. S. Eliot, in the essay on "Tradition and the Individual Talent" that he wrote in 1917, about fifteen years after *Tonio Kröger* and without knowing

Was Thomas Mann himself on the Lido at the time *Death in Venice* began to take shape? He was, in the spring of 1911; and had come there, like Aschenbach, only after he had tried out another seaside resort, Brioni (where he received the news of Gustav Mahler's death). Was there a boy called "Tadzio"? Very likely; a letter written to the author by a Polish lady explains, undoubtedly at Mann's request, the derivation of the name "Tadzio" that he had first perceived only as a strange sound. Did he write on the Lido a short piece of prose? He did, and the description he gives in *Death in Venice* of Aschenbach's little essay fits his own to a remarkable degree. Aschenbach had been invited to write something personal about a certain "cultural phenomenon." He was familiar with the subject in question and it meant much to him. All of a sudden, he felt the irresistible desire to write about it in Tadzio's presence and to let the theme shine with the notorious brilliance of his style. Thomas Mann's own brief essay, written in response to a journal's demand, was "About the Art of Richard Wagner" (X, 840 ff.), dated "Lido-Venice, May 1911." The manuscript, now in the Thomas Mann Archive in Zürich, was partly written on paper bearing the letterhead "Grand Hotel des Bains, Lido-Venice." Venice and Wagner: *Tristan und Isolde* was partly composed in Venice, and it was in Venice that Wagner died.

---

the story, joined that "fictional" German writer in his insistence upon the antithetical relationship between personal emotion and artistic accomplishment, while in 1921, about ten years after *Death in Venice*, he echoed, in his essay on "The Metaphysical Poets," Thomas Mann's contrary idea by postulating that poets should "feel their thought as immediately as the colour of a rose."

But the affinity of Thomas Mann's short essay and *Death in Venice* is of a still more intimate nature. The essay tells us that its author's love for Richard Wagner has always been a love without faith: he has never quite trusted the moral integrity of the enchantment. Yet this lack of faith has not diminished his love: "To me it has always seemed pedantic not to be able to love without belief." Mann then tries to define his relationship to the composer, and the definition gradually turns to lyrical invocation: "skeptical," he calls this relationship, "pessimistic, clairvoyant, almost resentful, yet passionate throughout, an indescribable seduction to live." And then

> Wonderful hours of profound happiness, enjoyed in solitude among crowds in the theater, hours tremulous with shocks of bliss, full of delight for nerves and mind, and of insights into things of touching and great significance as only this insurpassable art can yield.

Is this the way one speaks of a musical-theatrical experience? Or, rather, of sensations provided by Eros? "Touching and great"—this deliberately incongruous combination of adjectives Thomas Mann used again, on another occasion that would have some bearing on *Death in Venice*. In a letter of 4 July 1920 (to Weber) he calls "touching and great" the story of Goethe's falling in love, at the age of seventy-four, with a girl of nineteen, the story that Mann, under the title of "Goethe in Marienbad," planned to write in 1911 and which, as he himself said in his notebook, "became *Death in Venice*." But concerning the Wagnerian hours spent in the theater: put the beach in the place of the theater, and beauty in the place of art, and those sentences written by Mann on notepaper of a Lido hotel exactly describe the hours Aschenbach spent by the sea, passionately observing Tadzio, who, silhouetted against the infinity of sky and water, merged at the end with stirring, great, and significant memories of the myth: of Hermes, the beautiful guide of the dead (a god that afterwards acquired a kind of omnipresence in the writings of Thomas Mann).

There is, however, not merely an emotional connection between Mann's essay on Wagner and *Death in Venice;* their intellectual vicinity is equally close. For Mann's love for Wagner's art was not only skeptical, not only "almost resentful" and passionate; it also lacked belief—belief, above all, in the future of that art. Wagner, he wrote, was "through and through nineteenth-century," indeed he was "the representative German artist of an epoch" that will be remembered "perhaps as great and certainly as unhappy and unfortunate." When Mann tried to imagine what the masterpiece of the twentieth century would be like, he imagined something essentially different from Wagner's works, and "differing from them, as I believe, to its advantage." Such a masterpiece would be, he hoped, distinguished by its logic, form, and clarity; would be austere and yet serene; more detached, nobler and healthier than Wagner's operas: "something that seeks greatness not in the colossal and the baroque, and beauty not in the ecstatic." Unmistakably, it is Aschenbach's aesthetic ideal that Thomas Mann adumbrates in criticizing Wagner: Aschenbach's renunciation of the "abyss," of the inebriation of Dionysus, of the moral laxity inherent in all "psychological" understanding ("Tout comprendre, c'est tout pardonner"), and his singleminded dedication instead to a new simplicity and harmony of form which "henceforth was to give his productions such a deliberate stamp of mastery and classicism." This, then, is said in *Death in Venice* of Gustav von Aschenbach; and the passage from Thomas Mann's essay on Wagner ends with the prognostication: "A new classicism, it seems to me, is bound to come."—There can be no doubt left: *Death in Venice*, like *Tonio Kröger*, is a highly autobiographical tale, reflecting important developments in Thomas Mann's emotional *and* intellectual life.

2

"A new classicism": this marks the point at which the relations between the belief Thomas Mann has *expressed* in the essay as his own, and the belief he has *embodied* in the story, become most confusing and problematical. He may well have intended to write a "classical" work. But is *Death in Venice* an example, or even a promise and token, of such a conquest of the "abyss," such a recovery of classical simplicity, or such a "miracle of regained innocence" as, according to the "biography," came about in Aschenbach's art after he had left behind all those complexities of knowledge and understanding that inhibit or frustrate the classical moral resolve? Far from it. Mann himself seemed not a little baffled by the discrepancy between intention and result. It may be true to say—and he who says it can draw support not only from the essay on Wagner but also from the letter already quoted, to Weber, 4 July 1920—that he tried to adopt in all seriousness Aschenbach's classicistic diction. For even in the letter written almost a decade after the "classical" critique of Wagner and the publication, too, of *Death in Venice*, he says that it was his aim to achieve that balance between the sensual and the moral that Goethe had ideally accomplished in *Elective Affinities*, a novel which Thomas Mann remembers having read five times while writing his story. Is it likely that he did so only to learn the secret of the mature Goethe's prose style? No, also the theme of *Elective Affinities* must have been of the greatest interest to him: the tragic derangements caused by erotic passion, and the opposition between "civilization" and passionate "discontent," between the "garden" and the wilderness of nature. For this is precisely the clash that is also at the center of *Death in Venice*. Its every scene is vibrant with the shocks of the war between order and jungle, divine beauty and Indian cholera, serenity of mind and consuming passion, clear articulation and enticingly wild sounds of the "Panic" flute.*

Certainly, the experience that occasioned the story must have been passionate enough; Mann in his letter to Weber calls the inspiration for *Death in Venice* "hymnic," but continues by saying that his own artistic nature forced him to "objectify" the experience and thus to detach himself from it. Indeed, one may conclude that Mann himself at that time was assailed by the "Dionysian" spirit, a spirit "socially irresponsible

---

* To use a mythological shortcut: both *Elective Affinities* and *Death in Venice* tell of the conflict between Apollo and Dionysus; and it was Nietzsche, one of the young Thomas Mann's great educators, who made this tension between the "Apollonian" and the "Dionysian" the central theme of his celebrated book on the origins of Greek tragedy.

in its subjective lyricism"; that "extraordinary emotions," intoxicating and overpowering, seized hold of his soul; and that this soul tried to express itself "hymnically." Yet, disciplined by artistic restraint, what was meant to be an impassioned song became "a moral fable."—Goethe once expressed himself in a similar manner about *Elective Affinities* when he thought that he had to defend his work against a charge of immorality; and Thomas Mann wrote of *Death in Venice*, when he first mentioned the subject in a letter (18 July 1911, to Philipp Witkop), that it was, despite its apparent moral dubiousness, a "very proper" story.

The artistic preponderance of the Apollonian over the Dionysian, a new classicism, objectivity, restraint, the "ideal balance," such as Goethe had accomplished in his "moral fable," *Elective Affinities*, was recognized and affirmed by Thomas Mann; and this bears witness to his serious "classical" intentions. Yet the witness is unreliable. About a year before his letter to Weber, he had written another (6 June 1919, to Josef Ponten) in which he said, "Between you and me, the style of my story is somewhat *parodistic*. It is a kind of mimicry that I love and spontaneously practise." And on many occasions after this, Mann disclaimed as his own legitimate property the story's "hieratic" and classically measured diction, and drew attention instead to its "parodistic" nature.

Indeed, Thomas Mann employed henceforth, again and again, and ever more audaciously, this parodistic method whose secret is a premeditated and aesthetically mastered incongruity between the message delivered and the tone of voice in which it is delivered, between the outrageous tale and the conciliatory bearing of the language that does the telling. The outward literary gesture seems to ask challengingly: "Who, after this testimony, is prepared to suggest that the classical tradition of literature is seriously disturbed?", while the story, despite its being so decorously narrated, answers most emphatically: "I."

Nowhere is this kind of "parody" more successful than in *Death in Venice*, where content and form are at most skillfully arranged loggerheads. For the composition could not be more classical. It reflects what is *said* of Aschenbach: that he classically triumphed over the forces of formlessness and decomposition. Yet what is *shown* through this composition is the utter defeat of a classical campaign so disastrously waged out of season. The irony of this situation, profoundly moral and untouched by mockery, is Thomas Mann's way of acknowledging the tragically simultaneous presence of two incompatible forces within him: a conservative love of the classical literary tradition, and the disruptive insight that, alas, this tradition has had its day. It is once again the love without faith which, as he confessed, determined also his relationship to Wagner. *Death in Venice* conjures up, by means even of an occasional hexameter's intruding into the prose narrative, the memory of classical antiquity, but only to set against it the fate of an artist destroyed by the Beautiful in its catastrophic ambivalence: Aschenbach suffers his *Liebestod* by a sea as blue as the Archipelago, but dies in the vicinity of art's own city that has been ravished by the Asiatic plague.

It is through variations on the Platonic theme of love, beauty of form, and moral goodness that the tragic-ironical contrast becomes most lucidly articulate in three passages of the story, all of them purely reflective, and yet woven into the narration with great artistic intelligence. In the second chapter, Mann speaks of Aschenbach's achievement of that classical formal harmony in which the moral and the aesthetic are reconciled: that "miracle of regained innocence" with which Aschenbach so deeply impressed a generation tired of the "indecent psychologism" in which they had been brought up. Yet at once we read of "strange coincidences": how at the very time Aschenbach was about to achieve his new *ethical* certainty, his writings began to show signs of an almost immoderate and excessive *aesthetic* refinement. Could it be that the "classicist" moral resolution, made in defiance of those relativizing insights which apparently enfeeble the moral will, unwittingly strengthens the resources of evil? Does a man, thus determined, not refuse to understand and perhaps to cure moral ills? (Whoever, in later political episodes of Thomas Mann's biography, saw in him simply a conservative reactionary, or, afterwards, simply a progressive liberal, did not comprehend the meaning of *Death in Venice*, or recognize the vital and lasting part this problem played in his intellectual household: "Myth and psychology," his dominant preoccupation throughout the Joseph tetralogy, is only one of its many particular names, and "irony" its general one.) And aesthetic form, so the questioning continues, this necessary and foremost concern of the artistic will—is it not "double-faced"? Is form not at once moral and amoral (or even antimoral), moral because it is the expression and result of the artist's immense inner discipline, but amoral or even antimoral since by its very nature it is indifferent to morality, indeed intent upon subjecting the moral to the rule of the aesthetic? (It is a sign of this problem's force that what is said here of the *aesthetic* could, in this epoch of radically divided categories and loyalties, also be said— with still weightier emphasis—of the *scientific* in its relation to the ethical.)

The "two faces" of the Beautiful, presented together in these speculations, appear, each alone, in two later Platonic passages in which Plato-Socrates himself, the author of the problem, enters the scene, an enchanted and enchanting scene in the one, and an utterly disso- lute one in the other. In the fourth chapter, Aschenbach, already deeply in love with Tadzio, sees before his mind's eye Socrates instructing the youngster Phaedrus in the twofold aspect of beauty: beauty is both of the spirit and of the senses; indeed, it is the only form of the spiritual that we can receive through our senses and still endure. For would not the Divine, would not Rea- son, Goodness, Truth, if ever they revealed themselves bodily, engender a desire that would consume us like fire? This is why beauty, and only beauty, is our way toward the highest, "but only a road, a means simply, little Phaedrus."

For the last time in the story, Aschenbach maintains a classical control over the passions that threaten him with chaos. It is a victory won on the edge of defeat; and the closeness of the "abyss" is revealed by the words that follow, whether they are meant to express Aschenbach's thoughts or those of Mann himself. In any case, they are too "abysmally" psychological to be attributed even remotely to Aschenbach if we were meant to believe that he had genuinely conquered "the abyss" and forsworn every form of "psychologism."

Reducing to sheer psychology what for centuries has been looked upon as love's sublime wisdom, these words speak of the psychological "craftiness" of the classical suitor Socrates and of the ingenuity of the classically frustrated lover who comforts himself and fellow sufferers with the doctrine that divine is only he who loves, but not he who is loved; for the god dwells in the one, but not in the other. This Platonic thought, exalting the lover's love and at the same time diminishing the stature of the beloved, is, so we read, the source of exquisite erotic roguery as well as of the most secret pleasure of erotic desire. Where such psychological interpretations are practiced, there the rout of the classical virtues is at hand.

The motif recurs in the fifth chapter, near the end of the story, in the scene of Aschenbach's downfall. He has at last discovered the secret of the smell of disinfectant that pervades the city: it is due to the town's futile and secret fight with the epidemic of Asian cholera that is spreading through Venice. Although now Aschenbach knows, instead of warning the Polish family, he succumbs to outrageous fantasies: Venice and its beaches will be emptied by panic and death; only he and Tadzio will be left behind to taste "the advantages of chaos." During that night, the Apollonian artist Aschenbach has his dream of the terrible Dionysian orgy from which he awakens desolated, with the sense of his existence, the civilization of his life, destroyed. With his hair dyed and make-up on his face—cosmetically rejuvenated like that ancient "youth" who disgusted him on that ominous voyage to Venice—he pursues his idol through sultry and pestiferous alleys. One afternoon, exhausted by another vain exploit and plagued by thirst, he eats overripe strawberries, possible carriers of the deadly disease. (This is the second time strawberries make an appearance; they seem to play a role in the story not quite unlike that of the apple in the biblical Garden.) As he sits in helpless fatigue and frustration on the steps of a cistern in a dirty little piazza, the Socratic scene once more invades his imagination but in a form as deranged as is by now his own mind. Socrates speaks the initial words we heard before as he addressed young Phaedrus under the planetree: about beauty, which, at once divine and visible, leads the senses toward the spiritual. But then the classical meditation parts with its Platonic model and turns toward the abyss that now awaits Aschenbach, its "conqueror"; and Phaedrus is admonished to remember that "poets cannot be wise and dignified," that they "necessarily go astray" because their love of beauty is inseparable from desire, that the dignity conveyed by their style is "all lies and foolishness," their "renown and honor a farce," and that the education of the young through art is a "precarious undertaking which should be forbidden." Enacted with profound irony against the backdrop of an Apollonian grove near Athens, it is the intellectual consummation of Aschenbach's consuming nightmare, his vision of the Dionysian worshippers ecstatically dancing around "the obscene symbol," with the piercing *u*-sound of the flute, the Tadziu*uu*-call of the Lido beach, "sweetly and savagely" filling the air.

What establishes this Platonic theme of beauty, love, and moral goodness as one of the story's two most important leitmotifs is the fact that, sounded three times, it is almost the theme of the story itself, or at least a theme so close to the story's center that through its repetition, its variations and modifications, it seems of itself to tell the tale. This leitmotif, when first introduced, spoke of Aschenbach's single-minded dedication to the classical virtues of art, voicing at the same time subtle doubts: would his aesthetic sensibility be able to support his moral resoluteness? At its second appearance it alarmingly announced a precarious emotional involvement, yet soothed the anxious mind by delivering the classically restrained and restraining message Socrates has for Phaedrus in the Platonic dialogue. Its third "leitmotif" repetition, finally, signals the catastrophe: for now the classical text is as twisted and deranged as is, at this point, the mind of Aschenbach.

It was Thomas Mann's love for the music of Richard Wagner that made him translate the musical device of the leitmotif, so characteristic of Wagner's operatic compositions, into the language of literature, using it with ever greater subtlety in his novels and stories. In his first novel, *Buddenbrooks*, it is employed with epic simplicity, either in the Homeric form of the *epitheton ornans*, a characteristic of a person's appearance or manner that is repeated whenever the person is mentioned, or in the form of identical phrases that help the reader to recognize a significant similarity of recurring events or situations. In *Death in Venice* the leitmotif has both these functions to which, however, is added the ironical and weightier task of giving the highest degree of compositional order to this story of increasing disorder and decomposition. Like verse and rhyme in poetry, leitmotif speaks the language of form, and therefore of art, even when the speech itself says: form and art are done for. Mann's employment of the leitmotif may also be related to Nietzsche's "nihilistic" universe of the Eternal Recurrence, yet it reflects the hope, no less Nietzschean, that at least as seen through the eyes of art, the recurrent recurs because by some ultimate metaphysical ruling it has been found *worthy* of its ever new emergence, for this is the way the eternal comes to terms with the seemingly senseless operations of time.

Death in Venice is so thoroughly organized that its end is in its beginning, and from this beginning it is guided to its end by the other important leitmotif: that of death. On the opening pages Aschenbach is shown as, returning from a long walk in the country around his home town Munich, he is waiting for the tram on the periphery of the city. The halting-place is in front of a cemetery; and although Thomas Mann renders the locality and its neighborhood with faithful realism, his description soon becomes transparent for both Death and Venice to shine through. It is Venetian allusions that are conveyed by the "solitary glistening" of the rails; or by "the Byzantine structure" of the Funeral Hall the facade of which is "ornamented in luminous colors with Greek crosses and hieratic paintings"; or by the "two apocalyptic animals" guarding the steps to its portico; while the mysterious stranger, standing up there and attracting Aschenbach's attention, may belong to the domain of the Funeral Hall with its golden inscriptions that promise: "They shall enter into the dwelling of the Lord" or "The light of eternity shall shine upon them."

The strange man was "of medium height, thin, smooth-shaven, and noticeably pug-nosed"; he was red-haired and wore a "straight-brimmed straw hat" which made him look like "someone who had come from a long distance." He had a "knapsack . . . across his shoulders," and was clad in a "belted suit of rough yellow wool."

In his right hand he held a cane with an iron ferrule, which he had stuck diagonally into the ground, while, with his feet crossed, he was leaning his hip against the crook. His head was raised so that the Adam's apple protruded hard and bare on a scrawny neck emerging from a loose sport shirt. And he was staring sharply into the distance, with colorless, red-lidded eyes between which stood two strong, vertical wrinkles . . . Thus . . . his bearing had something majestic and commanding about it, something bold, or even savage. For whether he was grimacing because he was blinded by the setting sun, or whether it was a case of permanent distortion . . . , his lips seemed too short, they were so completely pulled back from his teeth that these were exposed even to the gums, and stood out white and long.

If we disregard—and the description of the stranger almost invites us to do exactly that—the meagre flesh, the little nose, the colorless eyes, or the almost missing lips, and only notice the white, long and exposed teeth, and his attitude as he leans against the iron-shod stick, which, a little extended, might serve as the handle of a scythe, then we have before us a Dürer image of Death. The reader will do well to impress the man's features upon his memory, for only then will he instantly identify the fatal stranger in the future disguises he adopts as the story proceeds: in the nauseating old man who poses as a young one on the deck of the ship heading for Venice, wears a yellow suit and a "rakishly tilted" straw hat, and willingly displays, when he laughs, a conspicuous row of false teeth; or in the

Charon figure of a Venetian gondolier who rows Aschenbach to the Lido, a man of exotic appearance, with a snub nose and a yellow sash who, when exerting himself with the oar, pulls back his lips and shows his white teeth; or, towards the end, in the street-musician who one evening is playing and singing in the garden of Aschenbach's hotel, a slightly built man of small features, pale and snub-nosed and red-haired with a strongly protruding Adam's apple. Here, as much as when it was mentioned before, the anatomical expression "Adam's apple" is, as it were, made to point back to its original, and, through a fascinating and a little dizzying linguistic action, reinstated in its literal *and* symbolic office: to remind us of the first man's encounter with desire and mortality.

These then are the leitmotif messengers of death that accompany Aschenbach on his journey; and this journey he *had* to undertake. The irresistible urge to do so came upon him when, exhausted by years of incessant and disciplined literary labor, he discovered the strange traveler by the cemetery in Munich. When he saw him, unaccustomed vistas opened which had the power of hallucinations. "All the marvels and terrors of a manifold world" tempted and enticed Aschenbach's imagination. There stretched before him a tropical swampland—fertile, chaotic, and voluptuous—the very place, it seems, where the Asiatic cholera has its origin and also the Dionysian dream of the strange, barbarous god, the dream that would complete the destruction of a mind once dedicated to Apollo, to the principles of sanity and lucidity. (It is a striking and telling coincidence of literary history that at about the same time that Thomas Mann wrote *Death in Venice*, Rilke began to write the Third of his *Duino Elegies* with its opposition of jungle and garden.)

If Thomas Mann had written, instead of *Death in Venice*, the work he first intended to write, the story of Goethe in Marienbad, "this painful, touching and great story which one day I may write after all," as he put it in the letter to Weber (4 July 1920), its theme would also have been, according to this and several other published letters, the fate of an artist overpowered by an "impossible" passion, a passion capable of afflicting soul and mind with feverish ecstasies, and the person with grievous and even grotesque humiliations. The story would have been of the old Goethe at the height of his fame, a European legend of poetry and wisdom, sage of *"Entsagung,"* of resignation and "classical" restraint, now passionately and therefore desperately in love with a girl of nineteen and in all earnestness proposing to marry her. It is obvious how much "Goethe in Marienbad" would have had in common with *Death in Venice*. Thomas Mann might even have exploited the subject's grotesque and humiliating possibilities beyond the limits of recorded biography: for instance, "Mama," the girl's "ambitious and procuring" mother, might have done her best to bring about the scandalous match, as the letter to Weber suggests. But in the end, the young Ulrike von Levetzow proved not quite right as the amorous occasion for utterly confounding the spirit with absurd promises of happiness and erotic delight. It had to be the boy Tadzio. Why? Thomas Mann's letter to Weber tries to explain how he came to abandon the plan of "Goethe in Marienbad" and decided to write *Death in Venice* instead. Yet he could not quite help hinting here and there in the

Venetian story at the neighborly relations between the poet in Marienbad and the writer in Venice. It would, for instance, be surprising if the two wax candles that, as the second chapter tells us, Aschenbach was in the habit of putting at the head of his manuscript, had nothing to do with the two wax candles that, according to Eckermann's *Conversations with Goethe* (27 October 1823), were ceremoniously placed at Goethe's desk when Eckermann was first allowed to see the manuscript of the Marienbad "Elegy"; or if the letter Goethe wrote to Zelter (24 August 1823) about the tremendous effect music had upon him during that Marienbad summer—it "unfolded" his soul as "amicably one opens and flattens a clenched fist"—were not responsible for the characterization of Aschenbach by a "sharp observer": " 'You see, Aschenbach has always lived like this,' and the speaker contracted the fingers of his left hand into a fist; 'never like this,' and he let his open hand drop comfortably from the arm of his chair."

What made Thomas Mann move his literary stage from Marienbad to Venice was, as he wrote to Weber, "a private and lyrical travel experience" which persuaded him to "go to the very limit by introducing the motif of the 'forbidden love.' " This explanation, despite its proper reticence, is clear enough; but it is probably not quite correct. Considering the extraordinary closeness of the two subjects, it would be surprising indeed if the idea of "Goethe in Marienbad" had not had its source in the same "travel experience" as *Death in Venice*. It is much more likely that Thomas Mann first tried to cover the all too autobiographical with the mantle of Goethe, and failed. "Lyrical experiences," while allowing their metamorphosis into literature, have a way of determining after their own will their degrees of revelation and disguise.

There is no other writer of his time who has been as conscious as Thomas Mann of the problems besetting the relationship between "life" and "art." His work gives the measure of this unceasing preoccupation. From *Buddenbrooks* through *Tonio Kröger* and *Death in Venice* to the novels of his old age, *Doctor Faustus* and, in its comic way, *Felix Krull*, this troublesome pair of opposites was never lost sight of. Whatever may be the "essential" nature of this relationship, its perplexities have certainly been considerably accentuated by historical accident or, if Hegel was right, by historical necessity. It was not by accident that the link, or perhaps, the gulf, between experience and its articulation, between the material of life and its artistic presentation, between autobiography and the literary work, has for so long attracted so much aesthetic philosophizing. The relation between art and life has become so strained, uncertain and problematical that ever more artists have, in their work, dared the flight into a sphere that is no longer that of life as it is actually lived and no longer shows or even demands a recognizable connection with the "concreteness" of human existence. Shunning the ever more difficult alliance with the "real," art has been tempted to settle where it is at last left to itself: in the domain of abstraction and pure form. Thomas Mann showed the daring, misery and fatality of this emigration in *Doctor Faustus*. His own work as a literary artist was determined by his profound awareness of this historical temptation and at the same time by his moral resolve not to give in to it; for such a resignation would implicitly dismiss life as something utterly unresponsive to the desire for meaning, order, or spiritual perfection, and thus declare it unworthy of the attentions of art.

From this inner awareness springs Thomas Mann's highly ironical traditionalism, which modeled itself on the classical products of literary history but at the same time could not help "parodying" them. The author who has so often been hypnotized by the "abyss" that had opened between reality and art, between the living self and the creative self, has yet in his ironical and "parodistic" manner succeeded in aesthetically redeeming much real autobiography through the medium of literature. A most exquisite example of this is *Death in Venice.*

BIOGRAPHICAL TABLE

1875   Thomas Mann is born on June 6, the second son of Senator Thomas Johann Heinrich Mann, in Lübeck.

1892   His father dies (born 1840). End of the firm of Johann Siegmund Mann.

1893   Becomes co-editor of a "monthly journal for art, literature, and philosophy," called *Frühlingssturm* (Spring Storm). Finishes his studies at the Lübeck Gymnasium and moves to Munich.

1894   Apprentice in an insurance company. Writes his first story, *Gefallen* (Fallen).

1895–1896   Studies at the Technische Hochschule (Technological Institute) in Munich. Contributes to *Das Zwanzigste Jahrhundert* (The Twentieth Century), a journal edited by his older brother Heinrich (born 1871).

1896–1898   With Heinrich in Italy: Rome and Palestrina. Begins to write *Buddenbrooks*.

1898–1899   Joins the editorial staff of the celebrated satirical journal *Simlicissimus* in Munich. Publishes his first collection of

	stories, *Der kleine Herr Friedemann* (*Little Herr Friedemann*) in 1898.
1900	Military service.
1901	Publishes his first novel, *Buddenbrooks, Decline of a Family.*
1903	*Tristan,* a collection of six stories, among them *Tonio Kröger.*
1905	Marries Katharina (Katja) Pringsheim. At the end of the year, daughter Erika is born.
1906	The "dramatic novella" *Fiorenza.* Son Klaus is born.
1909	The novel *Royal Highness.* Acquires a country house in Bad Tölz near Munich. Son Golo is born.
1910	Begins to write *Felix Krull.* Daughter Monika is born. Suicide of sister Carla (born 1881).
1912	*Death in Venice.* Begins to work on *The Magic Mountain.*
1914	The house in Munich, Poschinger Strasse 1, is built and occupied.
1915	The essay *Frederick and the Great Coalition.*
1918	*Betrachtungen eines Unpolitischen* (Meditations of a Nonpolitical Man.) Daughter Elizabeth is born.
1919	*Herr und Hund* (*A Man and his Dog*). *Gesang vom Kindchen* (Song of the Little Child). Son Michael is born.

1922	Fragment of *Felix Krull*. The oration "About the German Republic."
1923	Death of his mother Julia, née da Silva-Bruns (born 1851).
1924	*The Magic Mountain.*
1926	*Disorder and Early Sorrow.* Begins to write the *Joseph* tetralogy.
1927	Suicide of sister Julia, married name Löhr (born 1877).
1929	Nobel Prize for Literature.
1930	*Mario and the Magician.* The oration "German Address, an Appeal to Reason." Country house in Nidden, Germany, now Nida, Soviet Russia. Journey to Egypt and Palestine.
1932	Speeches and lectures during the Goethe Year.
1933	*Joseph and his Brothers: The Tales of Jacob.* Goes abroad, first to France, Sanary-sur-Mer, then to Switzerland, Küsnacht near Zürich, where he stays until 1938.
1934	*Joseph and his Brothers: Young Joseph.* First voyage to the United States.
1936	*Joseph and his Brothers: Joseph in Egypt.* Hitler's government deprives him of his German citizenship. He becomes a citizen of Czechoslovakia.
1938	Moves to the United States. Visiting Professor at Princeton University.

1939	*Lotte in Weimar (The Beloved Returns).*
1940	Moves to California.
1941	Builds his own house in Pacific Palisades and lives there until 1952.
1942	Political broadcasts to Germany. Consultant in German Literature to the Library of Congress.
1943	*Joseph and his Brothers: Joseph the Provider.*
1944	*The Tables of the Law.* Acquires American citizenship.
1945	Further political broadcasts to Germany.
1947	*Doctor Faustus.* First visit to Europe after the war.
1949	*Die Entstehung des Doktor Faustus, Roman eines Romans (The Story of a Novel: The Genesis of Doctor Faustus).* Suicide of son Klaus.
1950	Death of brother Heinrich.
1951	*Der Erwählte (The Holy Sinner).*
1952	Return to Europe. Decision to live in Switzerland. From now onward, annual visits to Germany.
1953	*Die Betrogene (The Black Swan).*
1954	First part of *Felix Krull, The Memoirs of a Confidence Man.* Acquires a house in Kilchberg near Zürich.
1955	Essay on Schiller. Speeches on the occasion of the 150th anniversary of Schiller's death. Dies on August 12 in the Kantonspital in Zürich.

THE PRINCIPAL WORKS OF THOMAS MANN

*American Editions in Translation
published by* Alfred A. Knopf, *New York*

ROYAL HIGHNESS: A NOVEL OF GERMAN COURT LIFE.
  Translated by A. Cecil Curtis   **1916**

BUDDENBROOKS
  Translated by H. T. Lowe-Porter   **1924**

DEATH IN VENICE AND OTHER STORIES
  Translated by Kenneth Burke. Contains Death in
    Venice, Tristan, *and* Tonio Kröger (*out of print*)*†   **1925**

THE MAGIC MOUNTAIN
  Translated by H. T. Lowe-Porter. Two volumes   **1927**

---

* Included in *Stories of Three Decades*, translated by H. T. Lowe-Porter.

† *Death in Venice*, translated by Kenneth Burke, reissued as a separate volume, 1965.

CHILDREN AND FOOLS
  Translated by Herman George Scheffauer. Nine stories,
  including Little Herr Friedemann *and* Disorder
  and Early Sorrow *(out of print)**   1928

THREE ESSAYS
  Translated by H. T. Lowe-Porter. Contains Frederick
  the Great and the Grand Coalition *from* Rede und
  Antwort; Goethe and Tolstoi; *and* An Experience
  in the Occult, *from* Bemühungen *(out of print)*   1929

EARLY SORROW
  Translated by Herman George Scheffauer (out of
  *print)**   1930

A MAN AND HIS DOG
  Translated by Herman George Scheffauer (out of
  *print)**   1930

DEATH IN VENICE
  A new translation by H. T. Lowe-Porter, with an
  *Introduction by Ludwig Lewisohn (out of print)**   1930

MARIO AND THE MAGICIAN
  *Translated by H. T. Lowe-Porter (out of print)**   1931

PAST MASTERS AND OTHER PAPERS
  Translated by H. T. Lowe-Porter (out of print)   1933

JOSEPH AND HIS BROTHERS
  I. Joseph and His Brothers [The Tales of Jacob]   1934
  II. Young Joseph   1935
  III. Joseph in Egypt   1938
  IV. Joseph the Provider   1944
  The complete work in one volume
  Translated by H. T. Lowe-Porter   1948

---

* Included in *Stories of Three Decades*, translated by H. T. Lowe-
Porter.

STORIES OF THREE DECADES
Translated by H. T. Lowe-Porter. Contains all of Thomas Mann's fiction prior to 1940 except the long novels 1936

AN EXCHANGE OF LETTERS
Translated by H. T. Lowe-Porter (out of print) 1937

FREUD, GOETHE, WAGNER
Translated by H. T. Lowe-Porter and Rita Matthias-Reil. Three essays (out of print) 1937

THE COMING VICTORY OF DEMOCRACY
Translated by Agnes E. Meyer (out of print) 1938

THIS PEACE
Translated by H. T. Lowe-Porter (out of print) 1938

THIS WAR
Translated by Eric Sutton (out of print) 1940

THE BELOVED RETURNS
[Lotte in Weimar]
Translated by H. T. Lowe-Porter 1940

THE TRANSPOSED HEADS: A LEGEND OF INDIA
Translated by H. T. Lowe-Porter (out of print) 1941

ORDER OF THE DAY
Political Essays and Speeches of Two Decades
Translated by H. T. Lowe-Porter, Agnes E. Meyer, and Eric Sutton (out of print) 1942

LISTEN, GERMANY!
Twenty-five Radio Messages to the German People over BBC *(out of print)* 1943

THE TABLES OF THE LAW
Translated by H. T. Lowe-Porter 1945

MODERN LIBRARY COLLEGE EDITIONS